FORGIVENESS

NEVER EASY/ALWAYS POSSIBLE

Healing

Rifts

among

Families,

Friends

and

God

FORGIVENESS

NEVER EASY/ALWAYS POSSIBLE

Healing

Rifts

among

Families,

Friends

and

God

A. KARL BOEHMKE

TWO HARBORS PRESS

Minneapolis

Two Harbors Press
212 3rd Avenue North, Suite 290
Minneapolis, MN 55401
612.455.2293
www.TwoHarborsPress.com

ISBN - 978-1-935097-79-2
ISBN - 1-935097-79-2
LCCN - 2010921027

Woodcut: "Homecoming" by Sister Marion C. Honors, CSJ
Cover Design & Typeset by Kristeen Wegner

Printed in the United States of America

To LaVerne

who has forgiven

seventy times seven times

and then some

TABLE OF CONTENTS

THE INN:
Four Miles from Nowhere

Darkness was fast closing in, that late summer afternoon as we headed our van westward through the mountains of Montana. To the north, the sky over Glacier Park had suddenly taken on an ominous cast, lightning flashing fiercely peak to peak; we knew we were in for a deluge. The campground at Kalispell had been our intended destination that evening, but it was becoming obvious we were never going to make it that far.

"We've got to stop," declared Abby firmly. "This road is so narrow, and these drivers refuse to lower their high-beams until they're right on top of you." I nodded, but then shook my head in frustration and mumbled, "We'll never find a place to pull in short of Kalispell."

For a time no more was said; we had no choice but drive on, rain splashing in blinding squalls across our windshield. We slowed to a crawl.

We had covered a scant ten miles more in unrelenting downpour when, wonder of wonders, on the grassy shoulder beside a dirt-road turnoff stood a neatly painted sign with shielded light above:

THE INN OF FRIENDSHIPS RENEWED
4 miles   Overnight Guests Welcome

Beneath the sign a metal tag swung wildly in the wind, on it the most beautiful word in the language:

$$\boxed{\textit{VACANCY}}$$

Together we heaved a sigh of relief and, van wheels spinning, skidded into the muddy lane.

The wind was gusting furiously, rain descending in torrents, as we carried our overnight bags into the lobby of the low rustic inn. No one was to be seen at the desk, yet a light was burning above the registry book. We heard a voice and the rattling of dishes from the dining room just beyond. Presently a short, balding man wearing a green apron over his camp clothes came hurrying out.

"I heard your van drive in; glad you found us, they say this storm is due to get much worse. Double room? Yes, of course. We've just about finished dinner but there's lots left — pot-roast tonight, all kinds of veggies and one whole pumpkin pie that hasn't been touched."

We looked at each other in disbelief.

"I'm Levi Matthew", the man went on. "That's not actually my name, but everybody calls me that. I'm maitre d' here, you might say jack-of-all-trades. Come on, sit down; you can sign in after the stories."

Still dripping small rivers from our jackets, we made our way toward the dining room, passing guests headed toward their rooms. "Seven-thirty, in the great room by the fireplace!" Levi Matthew called after them. "Right!" they called back.

In the dining room, someone had already set out fresh places for us. Hardly had we seated ourselves when the chef emerged from the kitch-

en wheeling a service-cart loaded with steaming dishes. We needed no second invitation. Levi Matthew had gone bustling off with a final word, "Seven-thirty, in front of the big fireplace." We weren't in the least sure what he had in mind, but whatever was about to happen, it looked as if we were to be in on it.

The guests had apparently gone to fetch sweaters and jackets against the cool evening air. Now they were drifting back into the great room across from the dining area and selecting places among the assortment of low sofas and cushions variously spaced about the room. Logs on the hearth were about to burst into flame as kindling licked at them from beneath. We slipped into chairs toward the back, while Levi Matthew propped himself against a rustic table directly in front of the fireplace.

"It's good to welcome all of you -- those here for the whole week and overnighters, too, I wish all of you could stay on." Then, with a nod in our direction, "A special welcome to our refugees from that wicked storm kicking up outside. Feel free to stay on as long as you like."

He paused, looking over the mixed group -- I would guess, thirty men and women in all, casually dressed.

"Sooo -- we are here to listen to stories, stories from the Bible, some forty of them in the course of the week. I shook the tree but lightly (he waved a Bible he was holding above his head) and these tumbled into my apron (he let the book drop into his lap). They all talk about forgiveness -- or the lack of forgiveness. 'Friendships Renewed,' is the name of our inn, and that is one pretty good definition of forgiveness. We want to recapture old friendships and restore broken families. Perhaps broken faith, too."

Some of the guests began readjusting their cushions. We sensed that somehow we were venturing onto sensitive turf. Levi Matthew went on:

"I don't have to tell any of you that forgiveness is tough going, one of the toughest things we attempt in life. Tough, yes, but possible. That is what these stories say to me — forgiveness is possible — possible for everyone. All of us can be forgiven, and all of us can forgive. Nobody need be left out in either direction. The two invariably go together, you can't have one without the other."

He paused once more, then, placing his hands on the sides of his ribs, audibly drew in a deep breath, then audibly let it out again. "What breathing is to our bodies," he went on, "forgiveness is to our souls. Breathe in, breathe out; breathe in, breathe out; physically we are alive; our bodies have the oxygen we need to function. Be forgiven, forgive in turn; be forgiven, forgive in turn; spiritually we come alive, our souls have oxygen, so to speak, to get along with our families, our friends, our bosses, our fellow workers, our neighbors, our enemies — to say nothing of getting along with God and with ourselves — which really come first in the sequence. It's a life-sustaining, widely encompassing process.

"A few of you mentioned, at the time you sent in reservations, that you find yourself unable to forgive some person or other; you wish you could, but just can't bring yourself to do it. Please be sure, I do not intend ever to refer to anyone or anyone's personal situation. No one need ever fear that I am talking directly to them or about them. The situations I mention are typical, universal. And they carry a universal punch, a punch aimed at those forces which drive human beings apart in the first place, but can themselves be proven vulnerable and, strangely, even useful.

No one in the room was moving now.

"Some sense their marriages slipping away; they've lost what it takes to communicate. One spouse decides to come to the Inn, or maybe

both. Some have gone through the heartbreak of divorce; they arrive here with shattered dreams, hearts sick, their vision of lifelong love ended in a nightmare of recrimination. Some have lost the trust of business partners or associates. On and on; any number of reasons why people find their way here. Some years back a junior attaché from the State Department in Washington, DC, spent the week here. She was on her way to high-level talks with tough bargainers overseas and wanted, as she put it, 'to just get my head on straight'. All kinds of people from all kinds of places, because these stories touch all sorts of situations.

"It's a complicated business, forgiveness. When someone you have deeply trusted betrays that trust, either deliberately or unintentionally, you cannot simply swallow a pill to bring trust back and heal your broken relationship. You hurt, and that hurt calls for deep therapy. Now, there are many therapists in many fields who stand ready to help. The past thirty years or so have seen deep study done in the area of forgiveness, and those doing the research have described for us just how interconnected and complicated is the web of relationships that links one human being with others — with siblings, with spouse, with clan, with nation, with cultures, with world — multiple, interlacing relationships, each atom of the universe somehow bearing on all the others. It's a complicated web out there.

"Here at the Inn we tell stories, stories from the Bible that have been told a thousand times before across the centuries. We believe that in the telling, and the listening, and the talking afterwards, and the listening to the talking afterwards, and the talking in the rooms evening or morning, or on afternoon hikes, or over coffee or Cokes on the terrace, something good happens.

"Some of these stories you'll recognize right off, maybe many of them. About others you may wonder: How did I ever miss them? To hear all these retold now in such a setting as this, and in the light of whatever special reason may have brought you here, holds promise of healing."

Abby and I looked at each other but said nothing. Of course, each of us knew about the other's former spouse and my two children, and something about what had gone wrong in our earlier marriages, but we had never talked about these in depth. To be honest, we were each afraid that if too much would come into the daylight too soon, somehow our new attempt at marriage would go poof. Each of us was vulnerable. But deep down each of us knew that eventually and inevitably things would have to be talked into the open. As we looked at each other in that moment, we could each sense what the other was thinking: "I need to stay and listen – that is, if you don't mind." And that was it: Kalispel and the remainder of our planned trip could wait. We would sign on for the full week.

Levi Matthew had paused to lift a burning log back onto the grate from where it had collapsed. He hung the poker back onto its caddy and looked up again.

"Now let me introduce Kori. Kori is a grad student at U of Montana; he has spent his last five summers here with us. Kori will be sharing the opening two stories about the Wayward Son and his Stay-at-home Brother. These stories most of you will recognize at once.

"And this is my lovely wife Rachel (he gave the lady at his side a hug) who has been trying to keep me out of trouble for 37 years. She will be telling the stories about the patriarchal families – the Wrestler, the Dreamer. Her own famous namesake, Rachel, appears in one of these.

"This distinguished gentleman sporting the chef's hat is Henri, our world-traveled master of the dining room. Born in France, Henri has spent years in Lebanon, Vietnam, Madagascar and a dozen other places; exactly how he found his way to this off-the-beaten-path lodge in Montana, I'm never quite certain. But considering the meals he serves, I'm thrilled that he did. Henri will be reading stories about the Kings and the Prophets— that maverick king who threw a big feast for his defeated enemies. Oh yes, and that stubborn Jonah preacher and

his problem, bigger than just being swallowed by a sea-monster.

"When we move into New Testament times, Lisa will take over. Dear Lisa — I'm sure you'll soon be calling her that, too — is in her third year toward a degree in psychology; her summers here are part of her field credit program. She will tell the stories about people taking stock of their inward motivations at the Jordan and on that Teaching Mountain.

"Finally, as Jesus of Nazareth recruits twelve special trainees, we'll meet one recruit named Levi, also known as Matthew. We combine his two names and ask 'Levi Matthew' to tell of his dealings and feelings toward Jesus and others, as if they are just happening. Now you can guess how I got my nickname— these are my stories to tell.

"To re-tell, I should say, for we are recasting these stories, which means we have fleshed out the brief Bible accounts with considerable setting, background, and often imaginary detail. the way an artist might do with the brush on a portrait. To check on the Bible stories themselves, you will probably want to turn to your own favorite version or transla-tion. You'll find one or another in each of your rooms, plus a whole shelf-full of translations and other helps in the reading room.

"For now, just lean back and listen. You never know what thoughts may be lurking. We are walking, as it were, along firm, damp sand at the edge of the sea. Preoccupied, we give scarcely a thought to the incoming waves. Suddenly an outsized wave rolls in and splashes over us, then slips quietly back out to sea. We stand drenched and shivering, shake ourselves dry and move on.

"So, Kori, if you please . . . ."

BOOK ONE

FAMILY

I. THE WAYWARD SON

A father welcomes home his spendthrift son.

I'm sure you have noticed how, within a single family, children often differ widely in personality. Maybe it is that way in your own family with one child shy, the other outgoing; one studious, the other all fun and games; one talk-talk-talk, the other you can't get a word out of her. That's the way it was with two brothers in the Spendthrift story that Jesus told. It forecasts and summarizes the whole Bible outlook on forgiveness — give and take, take and give.

One brother is the stay-at-home, the other all out-and-about. One is frugal to a fault, the other a spender from the word go. One is morally uptight, the other is, well, a swinger. Each finds the excesses of his own personality turn him into a stranger to his own home. Each loses the father and each loses the other. It occurs to us as we read how much of human existence con-

1

cerns drifting apart from people we love and from God. And then getting close to them again.

The younger brother is the active one, all verb. He asks his father for his share of the family inheritance, gets his way, goes off with his money, wastes it quickly in frivolous living, finds himself broke, looks for a job and can find none but that of swineherd — imagine a good Jewish boy employed as swineherd! — where he must vie with the pigs for the very slop in the trough. At length he comes to his senses, in desperation trudges barefoot the long, shameful way back home, determined to ask his father for a job as hired hand.

This young man has gone through a lot for his few years. I don't think he is a bad son, just an impulsive, foolish son. He has never really taken time to consider how much his father loves and needs him. His brother, too, for that matter. Now, inwardly chastened, he has his little speech ready on his tongue. But he is amazed to see his father come running far out onto the road with arms outstretched to embrace him. He begins his speech of penitence, "Father I have sinned against heaven and before you and am no longer worthy to be called your son. . ."

But the father will hear none of that. Instead he calls to his servants, "Bring out a new robe for the lad, new shoes for his feet, and a family ring for his hand! My son was dead and is alive again! He was lost and is found again!" He summons food and fiddlers and cries to his neighbors, "Let the homecoming party begin!"

Doesn't God want to hear about our shame? Doesn't God want to hear us tell about our wasted opportunities, our misused talents, our bodies neglected, our resources misspent? Of course, but not now, because God has already heard these much earlier than we might ever have imagined. Now God just wants us to have a decent bath, put on new clothes, be part of the family and community again. He just wants to hug us and laugh with us all the way to the house.

What a story! We cannot hear Jesus' Parable of the Wayward Son half-often enough. It is a good tale with which to begin; it both forecasts and summarizes the others. God's mercy is wider than all our faults even when we ourselves have finally discerned and owned up to them. God welcomes us home and clothes us with grace and newness.

This retelling is based on Luke chapter 15.

----

2. THE STAY-AT-HOME

The father welcomes home a son who never even left the farm.

What about that other brother, the older one, the quiet one, the stay-at-home? Jesus' parable goes on to describe his plight, too, and what a different person he is, what a different problem is his.

I picture him first at the time his younger brother leaves home with that share of the family farm jingling as cold cash. I see the older one shaking his head in utter disgust, "You don't know what you're doing. You'll go through it like water through a sieve, and you know how much we can use that money right here. Don't ever try to come crawling back, because, buddy-boy, everything is over forever between us two."

But now the younger brother has in fact come back and the older is out in the field where he has been toiling and fuming all along. He hears the music back at the house loud and clear, and no one has to tell him what that fiddling means. He was sure all along something like this would happen, and he knew that when it did happen, the old man would be stupid and soft enough to take the younger boy back into the family. Now things will be no better than before and all that hard-earned family cash wasted for nothing.

And who is this coming over the hill to persuade him to come inside and join the party? This father has left the house a second time within the day to find and bring in a separated son. "Your brother has come home and we've roasted the prime beef to celebrate!"

"I know well enough my brother has come home, and I hear the music loud and clear, and I can smell the roast in the oven, and I will never set foot in that house again so long as he remains there."

The venom all comes spilling out now: "I've served you all these years, yet you never even once gave me so much as a goat to have a party with my friends, but when this son of yours comes crawling home after frittering away our money on prostitutes, you kill the fatted calf to celebrate. Don't you care about our farm any more? Don't you care just a little bit about me?"

I don't think this brother is a bad son either. I doubt if he ever actually wanted a party, I doubt if he had many friends, or any friends at all. He is just a very human, self-righteous, self-pitying martyr type who has acted nobly over the years yet always gets the short end of the deal. If you tell him his heart is full of resentment, he will only remind you how loyal he has been. Here he is no more than a hundred yards from the house, yet little by little his heart has grown far away from his father, as far away as the younger brother when sloshing in that distant pig-sty.

And the father understands this, too. He knows it is just as possible to grow full of resentment at home as it is to go off and squander the family fortune in some distant land. He knows there are times when resentment has no place to go but to boil through to the surface. He does not argue: "Wait a minute, let us get a few things straight." He does not argue because his love for his elder son is equally as great as for the younger. He simply pleads, "Son, I know you're always with me. That's the way it should be. Everything belongs to you now. Only we have to spend a little, not just hold on to it. We have to take a little time to celebrate.

> *"Because if we are going to be living together we ought to be some kind of family."*

I suppose, it is harder to admit that we are this elder brother, too, not just the younger. We know we have been right for so long, should we suddenly admit that we may also have been wrong? Should we now be willing to take to our heart the person who has wasted the very things we have considered rightfully ours? How can God insist he really loves us when he receives felons, home-wreckers, and prostitutes into his house and then insists we love these people, too?

Strange, is it not, how ready we are to accept God's robe and shoes and ring at the moment we ourselves feel dirty and worn, but how resentful we become when God extends his grace to someone other than us?

At this point the parable in the Bible ends, but I like to think of it as going on, at least for another paragraph:

I like to think of the older brother relenting for the father's sake, taking his bath somewhere out in the stream, putting on his other clothes and slipping ever so quietly back into the house, then standing there quite awkwardly as his younger brother steps toward him, finally reaching out his hand and saying quietly, "Hello, little guy. Welcome home." And then something you might call a hug.

"Now, where, did you say, is that roast beef?"

This retelling is based on Luke chapter 15.

THE INN:
Clean Sheets!

We climbed out of our still-damp clothes into warm pajamas, Abby and I, then sat for a moment on the edge of the beds looking at each other, shaking our heads in disbelief. We had caught sight of a sign beside the road, and, suddenly, instead of having to pitch our soggy tent in the rain, here we were snugly housed and amply fed, listening to stories we had never expected to hear again at least not under circumstances such as these.

I vaguely recalled as a boy having heard that story of the Spendthrift Son and his Stubborn Brother, in a Methodist church school in the Boston Back Bay neighborhood. The leader who told the story had gone on to describe a man he met in the state prison who had listened to that story and it changed him then and there. He had confessed his wrongs to the chaplain and vowed to start over. Still for him at that time there was no new suit of clothes, instead the same old prison uniform for twelve more years.

Abby, too, could recall having heard that story as a very young girl. She had cried tears and clapped her hands when the spendthrift boy came home and neighbors came over for the party. The older kids at the church school had laughed when they saw her crying, and she had been hugely embarrassed.

As Levi Matthew had warned in his opening talk, you never know when an unexpected wave might roll over you, so we would listen but be wary of any memories that might be lurking. Levi's wife Rachel was due to share stories in the morning. Henri had added a word about hot cereal with honey and raisins, bacon, eggs and corn-bread with marmalade. Even if this would turn out to be just a dream, I hoped it would last at least through breakfast.

We climbed under the clean sheets.

----

3. STORM CLOUDS AT EDEN'S EDGE

"If we're going to be living together, we ought to be some kind of family."Rachel opens the Bible at the beginning to retell stories of the patriarchs.

Creation is newly finished and mankind has lost the garden home. In a chastened, bewildering world, a chastened, bewildered family must learn to make its way. Father Adam and Mother Eve conceive children; then all must learn to live as family.

Two brothers come center stage, again two brothers widely different in character. As boys we can scarcely tell them apart, tussling, wrestling, climbing, racing as children do, but presently we see them as grown men pursuing gainful occupations and here we sense their individuality. Cain, the elder, is a tiller of the ground while Abel, the younger, is a keeper of sheep. Yet it is not so much this occupational difference which distinguishes the two, as it is the attitude of each toward God, by which each seeks approval for his labor and in doing so lays bare his soul.

Each brings a sacrificial offering, selected from the rewards of his work. Sacrifice reflects both need and receptivity toward God. God, soil, Cain, brother Abel, their labor and responsibility toward heaven, earth, and each other intertwine in one complex act.

Abel's offering, chosen from the firstlings of his flock, is well regarded by God, whereas Cain's offering, chosen from the produce of his farm, is not accepted. Cain, furious at the divine slight, pouts that God is not fair. God explains: Cain's basic difficulty is evident enough: he is not living right. Sin, like a wild beast, is crouching at his door; either he must master sin or be mastered by it.

Cain chooses not to renounce sin; instead he becomes more and more its servant, and, correspondingly, more and more resentful toward both God and brother Abel. At last, in a fit of envious anger, Cain lures his brother into the field, attacks him, spills his blood, beats him to death. Mission accomplished, his rival is no more.

So soon violence and murder have entered the human family. They will never leave.

Throughout the story Abel utters not a single word. He simply lives righteously before God and dies at the hand of his aggressor brother. He becomes a symbol for the unnumbered innocent victims of violence throughout history whose daily lot is injustice. Cain for his part becomes a symbol for the oppressors and aggressors throughout history who solve their failure to relate responsibly to God, earth, and humanity by dealing violence to the righteous.

Yet the price for murder is to go on living in the sight of God, the desecrated earth, one's own conscience, and the eyes of the world at large. We hear the voice of God:

11

Where is Abel your brother?

How should I know? Am I my brother's keeper?

Of course Cain knows where Abel is. Of course he is his brother's keeper and knows right well that in this, his first responsibility, he has failed.

In divine sorrow God tells Cain he can hear the voice of Abel's blood crying to him from the ground. The very earth has been violated, Cain's bond to the soil profaned. He will indeed till the soil, but no longer will the soil generously yield its fruit. No longer will fellow humans consider Cain their brother. He will become a fugitive, vagabond, wanderer on the face of the earth.

In desperation, Cain cries out that such punishment is more than he can endure. Now the very soil, his livelihood, is against him, God is against him, all people are against him and will attempt to destroy him wherever he may turn. God says,

Not so! Whoever seeks to slay Cain will reap divine vengeance seven times over.

Vengeance is and must ever remain the prerogative of God the Creator, not of man the creature. Yet, vengeance once seized by mankind will become a curse to be borne willingly or unwillingly. The sword will in some fashion threaten every family and reduce every nation to its servitude. Mankind having grasped the hilt of violence must yield to the demands of violence.

God will put a mark on Cain to stay the hand of any would-be avenger. How or in what form that mark is printed on Cain's

12

person, we are not told. For the lady in Hawthorne's tale it will be a scarlet letter pinned on her by unrelenting townspeople. In our present story the mark of Cain is left for us to imagine. No need as yet to define its shape, for the Bible's long story is scarcely underway. Before the story is finished, that mark of Cain may come into clearer focus. It may even occur to us that we, too, somehow have worn that sign.

As storyteller, I will be bold:

Do you suppose that mark of Cain, imposed by God to stay the hand of the would-be avenger, might have been — could have been — *a cross?*

This retelling is based on Genesis chapter 4.

----

4. SEVENTY TIMES SEVEN TIMES

Hard on the heels of the first family's plight, comes a story seldom retold. With conscience-driven Cain we find ourselves somewhere east of Eden, in a land called Nod, a region not marked on charts, yet well-recognized by anyone who has ever struggled with conscience.

Five generations of Cain's descendents are traced for us along a single family line until we encounter Cain's great-great-great grandson, Lamech. Lamech's three sons are introduced as well — three sons with a triad of melodious names: Jabal, Jubal, and Tubal, each the founder of a branch of burgeoning civilization. Jabal becomes forerunner of Bedouin cattle raisers. Jubal is artist-musician, proficient on wind and stringed instruments, while Tubal subdues fire, enabling him to smelt copper and iron. One would suppose that a family possessed of such capabilities must surely prosper, but again tragedy stalks family and clan.

Lamech calls to his side his two wives, mothers of his precocious progeny, and confides, "I have killed a man in self defense." His words pour out in poetic lament:

Adah and Zilah, hear my voice, you wives of La-
mech, hearken to what I say: I have slain a man for
wounding me, a young man for striking me.

Such manslaughter, he insists, was involuntary. Still, he fears
his innocence will not deter the slain man's kin from mark-
ing him out for reprisal and death. He takes refuge in the
pronouncement of God made concerning his ancestor Cain,
desperately laying claim on his own behalf to sevenfold divine
judgment on those seeking vengeance — *except* that Lamech
multiplies that sentence by a hefty factor:

If Cain is avenged seven-fold, truly Lamech seventy-seven-fold.

Getting even, striking-back, vowing vengeance for vengeance
has become humanity's way of settling differences. Reprisal,
requital, retaliation, retribution, revenge, repayment in kind
will bedevil the human race throughout its generations. We
would prefer not to linger in Lamech country, did we ourselves
not recognize it so clearly.

Far along in the course of the Bible's unfolding narrative will
come a happier sequel to Lamech's lament, a story with a note
of redemption. For the moment we steal a look ahead.

Jesus of Nazareth, traveling the roads of Galilee, has called a
group of twelve men to train with him for a campaign which he
calls the Kingdom of God. The twelve have come out of various
families, tribes, and occupations and together are learning to live
as *"some kind of family"*. On occasion they succeed well enough,
but at other times, they snipe at one another, hurt one another and
wrangle. Until Jesus steps between them as mediator.

At such heated moments they know well enough what they are expected to do. They understand that loyalty to Jesus of Nazareth demands that they forgive one another and settle differences quickly. They have learned the advice of famous rabbis, that forgiveness must never be doled out in stingy fashion; forgive, if need be, seven times over. Yet is such patience fair? How much gaff should a person have to stand? Will not the offender continue to take advantage of your decency?

Simon Peter, one of Jesus' trainees, puts that problem directly to his teacher. Exasperated by some repeated offense, Peter complains "Lord, how often shall my brother sin against me and I forgive him, as often as seven times?" Simon, we suspect, has licked his feelings to the raw.

Jesus does not question the advice of sainted rabbis; instead he sets their bar many notches higher:

> Simon, friend, I do not say seven times, but seventy
> times seven times.

Quick now, good reader, how many times does seven times seventy times total up to? No, forget the higher math! Jesus' point is clear — don't ever give up forgiving.

God, you see, never gives up forgiving you.

This retelling is based on Genesis chapter 4 and Matthew chapter 18.

----

5. ROOM FOR TWO WITH VIEW

Among earth's burgeoning peoples, one tribe is chosen to bear light to the world. Abraham, founder of the race, faces up to the problem: who is to own and control the land?

It has been grim thus far – the Bible's picture of the human condition – but hold on, happier scenes come into view. Enter the Hebrew race, singled out by God to bear a torch of wisdom to the world. Abram (Abraham later on), a cattle-merchant, is founder of the Hebrew tribe. In Ur of Chaldees, city of his birth, this man hears the voice of God:

> *Go from your country, your tribe, and your father's house to the land that I will show you. I will make of you a great nation, and I will bless you, and make your name great so that you will be a blessing. I will bless those who bless you, and him who curses you I will curse; and by you all the families of the earth shall bless themselves.*

Abraham heeds the divine call. He travels, together with his wife Sarah, his nephew Lot, their combined families, employees, herds of cattle, and droves of sheep. Call it a migration of the prosperous, for Abraham is described as a rich man, the same being said of Lot. Their combined flocks and herds are so extensive that, were both families to attempt to settle in the same location, that spot must soon exhaust its resources.

We are not surprised to hear that strife has erupted between the herdsmen of Abraham and the herdsmen of Lot.

> *Look, we claimed this well!*
> *Go dig yourself another!*
>
> *We broke this new pasture-land!*
> *Now keep your stupid beasts away!*

An intra-tribal clash is in the making, a storm of passion which, if allowed to develop, may doom generations to come. Such is the course of recorded history. This Storyteller has read through an atlas describing the territorial holdings of tribes and nations from earliest human times to the present.* Page after page, paragraph after paragraph speak of unrelenting warfare, one tribe or nation wresting from another its holdings and resources – aggression and possession through the ages.

Yet the new race springing from Abraham's stock is called to demonstrate a new and better way. Abraham contemplates the growing tension.

> *We must not feud. We must rein in our herdsmen and settle these differences. The land that God lays before us is big— big enough for both. To separate will not be easy, but separate we must. If you take land to the left, I will drive my flocks to the right. If*

you take the right, I and my herds will go left.

The decision is squarely up to Lot. Eagerly the younger man eyes the Valley of the Jordan, so lush and well watered it reminds him of primal Eden itself. "That is for me," he declares.

Very well, I will drive my herds and flocks upland.

Were we to follow the younger man's career from this point forward, we would soon realize how unfortunate is Lot's choice – disaster lurks for him and his family. Yet that is not the direction of our search. For the moment we have witnessed a family kept intact through wisdom, consideration, and willingness to yield to the other. Abraham has proved himself an instrument of peace. Where he found ill-will, there he has sown love, where he found discord, there he has sown union. This man has discovered a formula by which human beings may learn to get along:

You choose the right hand, I will go left; you choose the left hand, I will go right. And God go with us both.

Do you suppose that in our world today there is space enough and resource enough for everyone: arable land, mineral resources, energy, food, everything it takes for human subsistence and prosperity? Would it be possible for every tribe on the planet to have a fair chance at a decent existence? What would it take to turn such a dream into reality? Wars are constantly fought to possess lands, lay hands on natural resources, control mountain passes, sea lanes, air-space, even outer space. Would it be possible to say, "The Lord lays before us a big planet, big enough for everybody. If you go right, then I will go left. If you go left, then I will go right?" That is to say, work things out equitably, so that everyone's need is recognized and everyone is offered a fair chance?

Later in the Bible, a writer named James will ask people to check their compulsive tendencies toward possessiveness. He will ask:

> *What causes wars, what causes strife among you? Is it not your passions that are at war in your members? You desire and do not have, so you kill. You covet and cannot obtain, so you fight and wage war. You do not have because you do not ask. You ask and do not receive because you ask wrongly, to consume it on your passions. Unfaithful creatures, do you not know that friendship with the world is enmity with God? Humble yourselves before the Lord and he will lift you up.*

The crux of human strife, as James perceives it, lies within our lust for the material and power to control it. He calls for putting the needs of others ahead of our own in the claiming of earth's resources.

James harks back to Abraham, founder of his race, homesteader of the spirit, pioneer for peace.

> *Abraham believed God and it was reckoned to him as righteousness, and he was called the friend of God.*

As the story closes, the two men, their families and workers share a farewell breakfast, embrace and go their separate ways as friends.

Abraham builds an altar to the Lord and offers a sacrifice of thanksgiving. As night falls, the voice of God is heard once more:

Indeed you will be a blessing, a light to the nations
of the world.

This retelling is based on Genesis chapter 13 and James chapter 4.
* Harper Collins, Atlas of World History, 1998, Borders

Abraham's Air

This land is your land,
this land is my land.
from the Great Rift Valley
to the tow'ring Highland.

From the Cedar Forest
to the Southern Waters,
this land was made
for you and me.

(parody, AKB, based on a lyric by Woody Guthrie)

----

6. FIRE ON MOUNT MORIAH

Hagar, maid-servant to Sarah and Abraham, bears this couple a surrogate son, Ishmael. When Sarah herself gives birth to Isaac, child of promise, she insists that Hagar and her son must leave. Profoundly shaken, Abraham endures a powerful test of family and faith.

Years pass. Again and again Abraham hears the promise of God that he will become the father of nations, yet he and Sarah remain childless. They determine to nudge the hand of God. Sarah sends her Egyptian maid, Hagar, to Abraham's bed and bosom to bear them a surrogate son. Hagar readily conceives and in due course presents her mistress and master a strong, athletic boy whom they name Ishmael — "God hears" — a name denoting hope and thanksgiving.

Yet more than a new child has arrived; jealousy and contempt have also come to crowd the tent. Sarah soon learns to despise the servant-girl who so eagerly bore their child. The maid Hagar, on her part, feels a claim on Abraham beyond her servant station. No longer can these two women exchange a decent, kindly word.

Years of family discord scar the boyhood of Ishmael. Now God, who looks beyond the fumbling of mortals, announces once more that the longstanding promise of a son and heir will be fulfilled. Abraham and Sarah, although far beyond normal years for conception, do indeed conceive the child of promise. In celebration, they name their new child Isaac — "laughter" — a joy to themselves and to the world!

Now, surely, Sarah will feel gracious toward all. Not so, for by now Sarah is so driven by jealousy that she must obey its bidding. No longer can she stand the sight or sound of Hagar and her despised boy. She demands that Abraham dismiss the servant-maid and Ishmael.

Abraham is torn between parental responsibility and his desire for peace in the tent. At length, wracked by guilt and anguish, this father-of-nations-to-be yields to the prodding of his wife. He will dismiss Hagar and the boy to become wanderers in the wilderness.

That scene of dismissal will haunt future generations. Canvases brushed by Hebrew artists will again and again depict Abraham's family torn apart by jealousy. Sarah stands defiantly in their tent-door, the infant Isaac clinging to her skirts. Hagar, the banished surrogate mother and her teenage boy, bending under the glare of Sarah's scorn, step into the fury of a blinding sandstorm. Abraham, anguished that his family should thus be torn through his own ineptitude, melts before the defiant glare of both women. In feeble frustration he extends one hand toward Hagar, the other toward Sarah. The boys cannot possibly comprehend the passions that drive them apart. Half-brothers by blood, yet enemies through circumstances not at all of their own making, when, if ever again, will these two live together in peace under one tent of brotherhood?

Hagar is banished, but has peace returned to Abraham's tent? Outwardly perhaps, but not within this father's tortured soul. Day by day he watches son Isaac mature into boyhood but cannot escape the shadow of his son Ishmael somewhere in the desert growing into fatherless manhood. Inwardly Abraham hears the voice of God telling him he must sacrifice Isaac, the heir of promise.

Take your son, your only son Isaac, whom you love, and go to the land of Moriah. Offer him there as a burnt offering on one of the mountains which I will show you.

The heart of the man recoils in horror. Pagan worshipers may strive to atone for wrongdoing by sacrifice of their young, but the One Lord God of Heaven whom Abraham serves has said that for him and his tribe there must be a better way. Conflict rages in the soul of the man until the matter be settled. At length Abraham can no more delay.

At the tent-door tears flow as mother and boy embrace in farewell. Father and son begin their three-day journey northward. For this far-traveled man this brief journey will be life's longest and most dreaded. To the boy's insistent chatter the father returns not a word, yet the firmness of his handclasp draws looks of wonder from the boy — so much to be talked about, yet so few words from this man lost in the toils of regret.

My Father, we have wood for the burning and live coals in the bucket, but where is the lamb for the sacrifice?

Boy, can't you see I am trying to pray?

The lad persists, finally the father exclaims,

My son, God himself will provide the lamb for the burnt offering!

Tears stream down the man's cheeks and his shoulders heave unrestrainedly.

Moriah, mountain of sacrifice, is reached, its summit gained and the sacrificial altar improvised. Abraham hugs his son one last time as he slips the rope about him. From the lad comes no word of protest. The knife is lifted and must be plunged.

In that moment, the voice of God's angel is heard:

Do not lay your hand on the lad to harm him, for now I know that you fear God, seeing you have not withheld your son, your only son, from me!

In a thicket close at hand a rustling is heard, a bleat, a ram struggling to break free of the bramble. The ram is taken and offered as sacrifice. In the smoky cloud, Abraham hugs his son, and the sound of their laughter echoes across the hills. Abraham re-names the spot "The Lord will Provide." More laughter there will be and feasting — oh such feasting! — when the two arrive safely home. Anguish and guilt have been assuaged by the grace of God.

Jehova Jireh

As evening falls, the angel of the Lord calls once more to Abraham. Trembling still for joy, he hears the covenant affirmed:

Because you have not withheld your son, your only son, I will indeed bless you. I will multiply your descendants as the stars of heaven and as the sand on the seashore. Your descendants will possess the gate of their enemies. And by your descendants all nations of the earth will bless themselves.

In the mercy of God, far-traveled Abraham has begun a journey more far-reaching than he can possibly envision. He has been handed a torch of redemption to be carried to the distant tents of humanity.

This retelling is based on Genesis chapter 22.

----

7. THE WRESTLER

A scheming mother and her conniving son conspire to cheat a brother out of his rightful inheritance. God intervenes in a manner that only faith can comprehend.

The son of promise, Isaac, has grown to manhood now and found himself a wife, the fair Rebekah. To this couple have been born two sons, fraternal twins, Esau and Jacob, once again siblings with personalities worlds apart. Esau, the elder and heir, is hairy, ruddy, born to the outdoors, your hunter-fisher type. Jacob, second-born by but a moment of time, is a delicate, refined, studious lad. In matters of business, Jacob proves himself ever the whiz, outmaneuvering his brother every time. Scholars speculate that the name Jacob means "trickster, schemer". Should that be correct, we may consider this younger brother well-named.

Rivalry between these two is more than normal sibling- squabble. The two are constantly at each other, wrangling, accusing, putting the other down. Things grow worse when Esau, anxious for a family of his own, brings two wives into the household, contentious women from neighboring tribes. Now no one can hear anyone else above the shouting and cursing, hardly the kind of household you would choose, were the choice yours to make.

Isaac, the father, fears he is about to die. Blind and infirm, he calls in Esau to explain that it is time to hand to his firstborn the covenant blessing received from God. "Go, hunt wild game for a ceremonial feast," he bids Esau. Rebekah, well aware of her husband's intent, has determined that Jacob, the younger, not Esau, shall become head of the family. Outfitting Jacob in some of Esau's hunting clothes, she prepares a dinner which Isaac will be unable to resist.

"That was a short hunt," observes the blind father, as he adjusts his napkin. "You *are* in truth my son Esau, aren't you?" "Yes, I am," Jacob brazenly lies. Thereupon the ceremony begins and the patriarchal blessing is pronounced. Jacob has been declared prime family heir and designated leader of the tribe of Abraham.

Of course, Esau's hunt was not that quick at all. In due course the elder son arrives back home, deer carcass slung over his shoulder. He shrieks in anguish as he discovers the fraud. "Bless me, too, father!" he pleads. Isaac will do what he is able, but there is no unsaying what has already been said. Such oracle as the trembling father does manage is small consolation for the defrauded Esau:

> *You will serve your brother, but when you break*
> *loose you shall break his yoke from off your neck.*

Esau vows that his day of breaking free will not be long delayed; as soon as Isaac dies he will murder Jacob, and thus rid himself of his hated yoke. Jacob, sensing his danger, flees northward toward distant Padan-Aram, home of his mother's brother, Laban.

The journey is one not to be forgotten. On a fearful night, as Jacob seeks refuge from storm and howling beasts in a rock-strewn ravine, the young man is granted a vision: God's angels flash earth-to-heaven, heaven-to-earth. Amid crashes of thunder the voice of God is heard reaffirming the covenant blessing. This schemer, this swindler — this Jacob — is affirmed by God as leader of the tribe of Abraham, bearer of the blessing!

We shake our heads. How can this be? This is unjust. How can God favor the scoundrel who has blatantly lied to deceive his own father and brother? Should God not rather have used those angelic bolts to strike the young man dead? Later biblical writers will shake their heads with us, as confounded as we. Their only answer: God is God. Who are we mortals to question? Were we somehow superior to Jacob in moral excellence, we might consider ourselves fit to sit in judgment on God and God's grace, but in fact we are not one whit better. God's grace lies beyond our understanding and is wider than our questioning. And only by that same grace are we free to lay our own sin at heaven's door once we have recognized and owned up to it. Such is the utter mystery of grace: God receives sinners and turns faulty human beings into better human beings. We stand mute before the mystery of forgiveness.

In Uncle Laban, Jacob meets his match at nasty tricks. He strikes a bargain with his uncle: he will work seven years for the right to marry his beautiful younger daughter Rachel. On their wedding night in the bridal chamber, Jacob lifts his bride's veil, to discover to his dismay that this time it is he who has been defrauded. He has in fact been married to Rachel's elder sister, Leah. Chastened but not deterred, Jacob serves another seven years to claim Rachel as well. From these two wives and their serving-maids are born eleven sons.

Recall if you will the wrangling that confounded Jacob's boyhood home. If arguing was the order back there, here it is even worse. Block your ears against the shouting between Jacob's people and Laban's. Jacob determines he must break free. Under cover of darkness, he slips away, guiding his two wives, eleven children and servants, extensive herds of cattle and flocks of sheep southward.

But now consider what he faces by returning home: the wrath of his brother who has had twenty years to nurse his determination toward revenge, his oath that he will break free.

As he nears Canaan, Jacob sends messengers ahead to his brother to say he has come begging for peaceful reconciliation. The messengers report back that Esau is advancing with 400 armed troops to confront him. Jacob now divides his family into two bands in the hope that if one band is wiped out, the other may somehow survive.

Rarely has this man Jacob prayed. Now, in a time of dire extremity, we see him sink to his knees to plead, "Almighty God, in mercy defend my loved ones, since I myself am powerless." He sends droves of cattle and sheep ahead as peace offerings to his brother. The driver of each is instructed to say, "These are gifts for my lord Esau" — ah, did you catch that title — *'my lord Esau!'*

Jacob stands at the Brook Jabbok. To ford this stream will bring him directly onto Esau's home turf. Quaking, Jacob embraces his wives and children, then sends them on across. He himself will stay behind long enough to pray as he has never before prayed. Through the long hours of the night he wrestles with a divine contender against whom he is helpless. He pleads that he might once again hear heaven's blessing. This time no angels flash. In misery, Jacob surrenders his soul.

What is your name?

Jacob.

No more. Your name shall be Israel —striver with God. You have striven with God and have overcome.

What? Swindler Jacob has overcome God? Hardly that — *overcome himself!* Overcome the demons that have so long controlled his soul. At long last he has begun to pray humbly and sincerely. He rises a new being. He has looked into both his own soul and the face of God. He has found divine courage, and now, come what may, will go to meet his brother. Born-anew, he splashes into the stream.

In the distance Esau advances in a cloud of dust with his four hundred. As the distance between them narrows, Jacob throws himself prostrate to the earth again and again.

Then, in a miracle of divine grace, Esau halts, dismounts, rushes toward his brother, throws his arms around him, kisses him!

God has melted the hearts of these two rivals. Together they weep tears of sorrow at years wasted in mutual hatred and tears of joy at brotherhood renewed.

Canopies are thrown up and made ready for the feast. Brothers look on as families intermingle with long-wished-for hugs and squeals of delight. It occurs to them now that the oracle wrung a score of years ago from the lips of their father Isaac has indeed been fulfilled, the yoke flung off -

> *that cursed yoke of hatred,*
> *that shameful yoke of deceit,*
> *that despised yoke of servitude,*
> *that damnable yoke of plotted vengeance –*

torn off and cast away. The grace of God has set free both their hearts.

This retelling is based on Genesis chapters 27-33.

----

8. THE DREAMER

Ten brothers sell their younger half-brother into slavery, yet the grace of God converts their cruelty into survival for the tribe. For the first time in the Bible we encounter the word 'forgive'.

Twelve sons of varying ages crowd Jacob's family camp. Ten are children of Leah, Jacob's first wife and her maid. The remaining two are sons of Rachel, the younger bride. These younger brothers are motherless now, for Rachel has died giving birth to Benjamin, the twelfth and last.

It is Rachel's older son, Joseph, whom father Jacob chooses as his all-too-obvious favorite. You might think that sad experience from his own childhood would warn Jacob to beware the pitfalls of favoritism. Hardly so, the man seems unaware as he heaps gift after gift on Joseph. He outfits the lad with a tailored robe, that famous coat of many colors with fancy sleeves, the day-by-day envy of the ten older half-brothers who take unkindly to their father's favoritism.

Were this not sufficient cause for resentment, young Joseph on his own begins to dream about assuming an exalted position in the family. At supper, he is naive enough to relate his dream to the family: a harvest field where the brothers' sheaves of wheat bow down before his own sheaf. The father tries to hush the boy, but the lad persists. Soon, the enraged brothers begin to talk of putting their half-brother out of the way, awaiting only the proper moment and circumstance.

The moment arrives in the remote summer pasture where the older brothers have driven the family flocks. Young Joseph is due to arrive carrying in supplies. From a distance the brothers spot that hated coat. "Now!" But older voices urge restraint, and when a caravan of traders bound for Egypt passes close by, the brothers strip Joseph of his coat and sell him into slavery. As for the hated garment, that they dip into goat's blood and carry back as evidence to their father. "The lad must have been attacked and eaten by some wild beast." Jacob shrieks, then enters a month of mourning for his lost son.

Alive and well in Egypt, Joseph has been re-sold to the commander of the pharaoh's bodyguard. So impressed is this officer with the young man's abilities that he entrusts his household management to him. When the commander's wife propositions Joseph and the young man turns down her advances, she accuses him of attempted rape and sees that he is sentenced to prison.

Even in prison, fortune smiles. Joseph correctly interprets the dreams of palace employees awaiting trial; soon his talents become recognized in the royal court itself. There, pharaoh has been troubled by a disconcerting dream:

Seven skinny river-cows eat up seven plump river-cows, yet for all their eating grow scrawnier still. Joseph interprets this dream in economic terms; seven years of bumper harvest lie ahead, beyond these seven years of famine. "Find an overseer,"

Joseph counsels, "to buy and store great quantities of grain against impending shortages and run-away prices."

To whom should the position of overseer be offered but to Joseph himself? People are amazed to see a young Hebrew wielding power in Egypt second only to the king. Joseph rides a royal chariot out to the wheat fields to purchase great quantities of grain at low prices for storing in royal storehouses.

When lean years arrive, no one is spared, certainly not neighbors in nearby Canaan. Father Jacob must send his ten older sons to buy Egyptian grain.

At the granary, the Egyptian-Hebrew overseer can scarcely believe his eyes. Can these visitors be his very own half-brothers? For their part the brothers have no way of identifying Joseph. Joseph instructs his workers, "Put the Hebrews' purchase money back into their sacks, then have exit guards charge them with theft." In the court he offers the brothers a hearing, then allows them to leave Egypt on condition that one remain behind as hostage; if ever the others visit again, they must bring their youngest half-brother, Benjamin, with them. Judah is held in prison.

Back in Canaan Father Jacob is distraught. Under no circumstance will he allow Benjamin to leave home. Yet pangs of hunger will not remain silent. Again the brothers must venture south, this time with Benjamin in their sworn keeping. A second time grain is purchased. This time, by Joseph's order, the royal silver drinking goblet is planted in Benjamin's sack. The border police apprehend the lad, charging him with high misdemeanor.

Now the older brothers are reduced to absolute terror, standing as they do between a court trial here and their father's imagined wrath at home. "Punish any one of us," they plead, "only let Benjamin go free." Whereupon Joseph can play his charade no longer. He reveals himself to his brothers who stand utterly dumbfounded, reduced to trembling and tears at this incredible turn of events.

Joseph, at pharaoh's pleasure, invites aged Jacob and his entire household to migrate, flocks and all, to Egypt, to the most fertile grazing area of the entire land. Seventy souls complete the journey.

At length it is time for aged Father Jacob to die. Once again Joseph's brothers quake. Perhaps it was only out of regard for their aged father that Joseph has treated them so decently. Perhaps now this brother, before whose shock of wheat their own sheaves have indeed bowed down, will take revenge on them for their ill treatment. They compose a letter in which for the first time in the Bible the word 'forgive' is recorded.

> *Honored Sir, we pray you, forgive the sin of the children of your father.*

Revenge is the farthest thing from Joseph's mind. Instead, he arranges a feast where the half-brothers weep and exchange words of reconciliation. Joseph is astonished:

> *Am I in the place of God? You intended evil against me, but God intended it for good, that our entire family might be preserved alive.*

The miracle of divine grace has prevailed. Favoritism, envy, jealously, reprisal have melted away under the warmth of God's mercy.

With that, the Book of Beginnings draws to its close. Yet we must not leave without remarking on how often families re-discover love for one another in the extremity of death and mourning.

Brothers, sisters, cousins, in-laws, friends have not spoken to one another in years, held apart by grievances they can honestly no longer recall. They receive the message: "Mother has died." Of course, each will attend the funeral. There beside the coffin of their loved one, they come face to face with each other once again. They look into each other's eyes, shake each other's hand, embrace awkwardly and weep. They hear a minister recall mercies of God shared during the life of the deceased. "Why have we not spoken and visited for all these years?" they ask themselves. "Mother would want us to begin again."

Then suddenly it is time to catch planes. "We must write, we must call, we must e-mail, we must visit." Wounds of long standing have been looked at and attended to.

Their planes gain cruising altitude. They settle back. They have lost a loved one, but their gain is far greater. The hand of God moves in mysterious ways. It had never occurred to them as they left home, that God intended this trip for the good of many.

This retelling is based on Genesis chapters 37-50.

THE INN:
Rogue Wave on Cobblestone Terrace

Rachel concluded her stories. Henri announced supper to be served on the cobblestone terrace back of the Inn. He reminded us that his own set of stories was due to start by the great fireplace in just a few minutes. Abby was already helping gather up dishes, heading indoors along with the others. I asked would she mind if I would sit by myself a bit longer to watch the sun go down. She did not mind and continued on in to find a spot near the fireplace.

I will share with you, good reader: That rogue wave which Levi Matthew warned us about had hit me and left me dazed and drenched. I had told myself a dozen times such a thing must never happen, would not happen, but rogue waves, it appears, do not ask permission.

Rachel's story about Hagar and Sarah had done it – that pathetic scene showing those two women Hagar and Sarah and their boys Ishmael and Isaac, glaring at each another, with husband Abraham standing distraught in the middle. I suddenly was flashing back to Allison and the girls, and Abby, with myself caught limp in the middle.

When that connection first went through my mind, I said, "Utterly ridiculous!" Sarah and Hagar in the story had been living together in that same tent for a dozen years and had been daily at each other's throat, while Allison had never so much as known that Abby even existed until five full years after the divorce became final. And then only by accident that day she and the girls ran into Abby and me at the mall and I made that awkward attempt at introducing Abby as though we were just casual friends. There never could have been words between those two women; I had managed to keep them separate even in my own mind.

Yet here I was feeling as helpless as Abraham on that day he sent Hagar and her son out into the desert storm. To be honest, I, too, had nudged the hand of God — had gone to Allison's parents, arguing that we were both mature well beyond our ages of 18 and 17. Would they give their consent to our marriage? They simply must. They had reluctantly agreed, and both families had turned out in force for the church wedding, complete with tuxes and formals, rehearsal supper, reception banquet, gifts, all the trimmings. Our marriage had gone smoothly enough for a time, but it quickly turned sour, far quicker than I would have believed possible.

Our quarreling boiled down to this: I had my career plans and Allison wanted babies. I insisted nothing must interfere with my road trips that would put me in better position for promotion, while she insisted that I owed more time and effort to getting a family started. That we actually allowed ourselves to bring both Jamie and Julie into the world within two years time under such tension, I still find hard to believe, but that we did.

I was flabbergasted when I learned that Allison had been spending nights with Rod, my life-long buddy. I refused to believe such a thing was even possible, and here it had already been going on for months. I was bitter, bitter, bitter. That next year until our divorce became final was the toughest year of my life. And during the years after that, my bitterness turned to contempt, especially toward Ron. I swore to God I could never forgive either him or Allison — or myself for that matter — or God, for all the good that God and the church had done us. "Winchester Cathedral, you're lettin' me down, you stood and you watched as my baby left town." I vowed never to make the mistake of marrying again.

And then I met Abby at the company picnic where I had taken the girls on our once-a-month visiting day. Something had resonated between the two of us, Abby and me. When I asked whether I might see her again, she had agreed. Then she immediately told me about her own messy divorce and how determined she was never to let such a thing happen again. We found ourselves seeing eye-to-eye on so many things, physically hungry for each other, and head-over-heels in love. We agreed, whatever our earlier circumstances had been, they must never be allowed to threaten our new relationship. Soiled linen could be kept well out of sight for now, time enough for sorting that out later on. For now just getting off to a solid beginning was what mattered. A dozen close friends had gathered, three weeks ago at Scranton City Hall where a justice of the peace heard us say our vows.

So here we were honeymooning, Abby and me, agreed that the past must remain past, listening to stories that must have nothing to do with our own stories.

Until that blasted rogue wave!

Somebody was sending two young girls out into the sandstorm of sub-teen years, and that somebody was me. Two precious girls who should never have started calling that bastard Rod their daddy. And yes, my career is that important — important enough to let a poorly managed marriage go to ruin. And yes, I think I really do have the stuff now to be the kind of husband Abby wants and deserves. And no, that stupid rogue wave has not left me limp as Abraham at his tent door. Well, if it has, I have every right to feel this way.

Why should I even allow these thoughts into my mind? We never made reservations for this crazy place or agreed to this kind of mental going over. This whole damn situation is getting ridiculous. It has got to be a bad dream; high time to shake myself awake and get us out of here.

The brief autumn sun had plummeted behind the mountain. The flicker from the great fireplace was already shimmering on the firs behind the Inn. I could faintly hear Henri's old-world brogue as he launched into his stories. Damn, damn! I slapped the arm of the deck-chair hard enough to make my wrist sting.

Then I shoved the chair back and moved quietly inside to join Abby. She was carefully guarding an extra cushion at the very rear of the great room. Without turning she reached out for my hand and held it for a long time, while I struggled to get my mind in sync with Henri's new stories.

Then, as if startled, Abby turned and looked questioningly into my eyes.

BOOK TWO

NATION

9. A NEW NATION UNDER GOD

In the Sinai Desert a new nation is conceived and born. Its charter binds God to people, people to God, and people to each other.

The mountain called Sinai is a raging inferno. Smoke and fire belch from its crater, while lightning stabs incessantly through the blackness of enveloping clouds. The whole region heaves and groans, as for miles around the earth shudders. Furious winds tear at rocky crags, sending boulders crashing into the valleys below, their shriek echoing through the defiles like the blare of some cosmic trumpet. In the midst of such fury a lone figure makes his way upward into the heart of the conflagration, a man intent on hearing a message from God – a message he believes will inspire the building of a new nation and ultimately a new world.

At the foot of Sinai, trembling with the quaking earth itself, a band of ex-slaves cower in fear. These are escapees who weeks before fled the whips of their Egyptian taskmasters. Here in the barren wastes of Sinai they fear once more for their lives. When their leader completes his strange journey, they are to become a truly liberated people, called to a task no less than re-shaping the course of the world's history.

Four hundred years have passed since the days of Joseph and his brothers. The family of Israel, living in Egypt, has multiplied in numbers but not in fortune. They have, in fact, been enslaved for generations by the royal House of Pharaoh. These Children of Israel, as we call them now, must endure hard labor and bitter living conditions. The Egyptian royal house, fearing their rapid numerical increase, has decreed that newborn Hebrew males be killed by drowning in the Nile.

An Egyptian princess, hearing a tiny cry from a basket floating amid the reeds where she is bathing, rescues a baby boy, names him Moses, and raises him as a royal prince in the palace. Grown to manhood, Moses learns of his Hebrew heritage and vows that he will set his people free from their enslavement. When, in a fit of anger, he strikes and kills an Egyptian slave-master, he is forced to flee into exile in the Sinai desert. There on the mountain called Sinai (or Horeb), he hears the voice of God speaking out of a burning bush. God has not forgotten his Chosen People. This is the message Moses hears:

> *I am the God of your fathers, the God of Abraham,*
> *Isaac, and Jacob. I have seen the affliction of my*
> *people and heard their cry. I have come to deliver*
> *them and bring them to a land flowing with milk*
> *and honey. Come, I will send you to Pharaoh.*

When Moses strides into the court of Pharaoh, demanding that his enslaved countrymen be allowed to worship God in the desert, Pharaoh only scoffs. Whereupon the land of Egypt suffers a series of devastating plagues: drinking water contaminated, swarms of frogs, gnats, locusts, ruinous hail, unnatural darkness. For Pharaoh such disasters carry no message of divine judgment; each calamity makes him that much the more stubborn. He orders the Hebrew slaves' labor be made more intensive.

Until one fateful night — that night long to be remembered as Passover — when the angel of death enters Egyptian homes claiming the life of each eldest son. Hebrew homes the angel 'passes over,' since householders, at Moses' order, have painted their doorposts with the blood of a lamb.

Terrified at such loss, Pharaoh, his own dead son limp in his arms, relents for a brief hour, time enough for the Israelites to flee helter-skelter into the desert. Then, his stubbornness revived, Pharaoh commands his royal charioteers to pursue the fleeing slaves and to hack them to pieces in the sand. The escapees, trapped at the shore of the Sea of Reeds, appear doomed, but a mighty east wind springs up, driving the water of that shallow sea clear out of its bed. In the shrieking wind, Moses and the fleeing slaves safely cross the seabed. Then, as suddenly as it arose, the wind dies and, with a mighty roar, the water is sucked back into its accustomed seabed. The charioteers of Egypt, struggling to free their wheels from the sand, are trapped and drowned in the returning surge.

In utter awe at such divine deliverance, Moses and his people flee eastward, drawn toward Horeb, the volcano wrapped by day in smoke, by night afire. At the quaking base of that mountain they pitch their camp, while Moses begins his ascent into the inferno, once more to hear the voice of God:

> *Tell the people of Israel: If you will obey my voice*
> *and keep my covenant, you shall be my own posses-*
> *sion among all peoples; for all the earth is mine, and*

you shall be to me a kingdom of priests and a holy
nation.

Moses listens as the ancient call to Abraham is renewed. The heirs of the patriarchs are about to become a blessing to the earth. Freed from the bondage of Egyptian whips, they will become heralds of redemption for the oppressed peoples of the world.

For that they will need a more explicit charter, a broader constitution, a moral foundation on which to build their nation. Call this the Torah, heaven's law for the new nation. In just a few hundred introductory words – then in fifty thousand more — the Torah will sketch out the structure of the nation-to-be. These people will see themselves as instruments of God. They will enter and occupy a land of vast physical and moral potential.

Down from the mountain comes Moses, carrying in his arms two tablets of stone –Tablets of the Torah intended to shape the people's future. From the first tablet he reads:

> *I am the Lord, your God, you shall have no other*
> *gods before me. Do not fashion for yourselves the*
> *likeness of any creature to bow down to or to serve.*

> *Do not take the name of the Lord your God in*
> *vain.*

> *Remember the Sabbath Day to keep it holy. Each*
> *seventh day will be a day of rest dedicated to the*
> *Lord your God.*

Out of such initial reverence for God, creator of the world and ruler of the the nation, all activity must flow. All human relationships whether in family, community, or nation-at-large, will draw their bonding power from common reverence toward God. Hence, the Second Table, defining other relationships:

Honor father and mother.

Commit no murder.

No adultery.

No stealing.

No false witness toward neighbor.

No coveting of a neighbor's belongings –house, spouse, servants, goods – not a thing that is his.

On the bedrock of these brief principles Israel's tribes may live successfully with God, successfully with each other and honorably in the world:

You will live long in the land which the Lord your God gives you.

In the wake of these Ten Commandments comes a lengthy collection of ordinances and by-laws, dealing with the structure and responsibilities involved in human relationships. Each relationship functions with light and power flowing out of the basic commandment, *I am the Lord your God.* Families, tribes, communities will be tied to one another, then webbed together, by the same cords which bind them to God.

Love God above all.
Love neighbor as self.

So begins the experiment of the ages: former slaves endeavoring to build a new nation grounded and founded on the principle of love. Can such an experiment possibly succeed?

Forgiveness will be called for at every turn.

This retelling is based on Exodus chapter 20.

----

10. PROMISES! PROMISES!

Make a promise — quite easily done.
Keep a promise — ah, that is another matter.
Make a promise — you are putting your character on the line.
With time, you will reveal what kind of person you are.

Promise to marry 'til death do you part, promise to pursue a demanding calling, promise to care for a child or some aged soul, promise to pay bills on time, promise to be a worthy citizen. On and on, a thousand promises. With each promise you acknowledge responsibility and enter into a contract, formal or informal, with God and with the fellow beings to whom your promises have been made. And since at best you are but human clay, you will need the power of forgiveness to see you through.

On Mount Sinai Moses has received the divine promise: God will turn this hapless, shapeless band of ex-slaves into a nation of kings and priests to bless the whole earth. Comes now the question: Are these people willing to assume responsibility so immense? At the foot of the smoking mountain an unforgettable scene takes place.

At Moses' summons, the whole band of escapees, twelve tribes bearing the names of Israel's sons, have assembled. From stones which litter the desert floor Moses has erected twelve pillars to symbolize the new confederation, shafts tall enough to be seen throughout the camp. Silently these rocky pillars announce: We are now one new nation! Among these pillars Moses has erected an altar and on this altar has prepared an offering: twelve oxen slain for the burning. Before going further, Moses reserves the blood of the beasts in large basins.

Soon smoke from the sputtering sacrifice begins to rise, mingling with ash sifting from Sinai's crater and drifting across the anxious onlookers. In a bold, dramatic move, Moses lifts the basins and splashes half of the reserved blood against the stones of the altar. As blood drips from altar to earth, Moses shouts: "The slave pits of Egypt are forever left behind; now we build a nation to startle the world with righteousness. Are you willing to accept the Law of God as your own? Can you be counted on to bear such high responsibility?"

From the crowd a roar of assent rises : "Yes! Yes! Everything that God has declared we will do! We will be obedient!"

> *Make a promise — quite easily done.*
> *Keep a promise — ah, that is another matter.*
> *Make a promise — you are putting your character on the line.*
> *With time, you will reveal what kind of person you are.*

Moses does not intend that the people should forget that to which they have committed themselves. Half of the sacrificial blood, you will recall, remains in those basins. Seizing those vessels once more, Moses flings the remainder of that blood out over the heads of the people. *"See,"* he shouts, *"the blood of the covenant which the Lord has made with you by giving you these words!"* The spattering blood can scarcely reach every last soul in that assembly, yet the sight and shock of this bold action will leave no soul unmoved. All will remember what they have heard and seen, and how they have responded. With that, the pact is both signed and sealed, the great experiment underway. Can a nation of liberated slaves fulfill such high destiny?

Back to the high plateau goes the climber Moses, this time accompanied by Joshua, his aide-de-camp and successor-to-be. They will focus now on the by-laws, the ordinances, which will lend structure to the new nation. The two will be away from camp for six weeks.

Down in the camp the people soon grow restless. They are not accustomed to dealing with a god who cannot even be seen. Back in Egypt there were all sorts of images — half-human beasts and birds — before which worshipers might bow, celebrate, sing and dance. "Make us a god!" they shout to Moses' brother Aaron, the camp *charge d'affaires*.

Eagerly they give Aaron gold earrings, bracelets and other such booty carried away from Egypt. Later Aaron will sheepishly explain to Moses that all he did was drop the peoples' gold into the smelter's pot and out came this calf spontaneously. God does wonderful things, you know; no harm meant. And, after all, people do require some visible presence to lend substance to their worship. Moses, however, will not be amused.

In fact, Moses and Joshua are coming off the mountain now, arms loaded with tablets containing the fleshed-out law, their minds swimming with bold social ventures for this nation-to-be. As they approach the camp they can scarcely believe what they hear: the sound of music, drums, and dancing. It takes but one glance to convince them what has been going on. As they catch sight of the golden calf gleaming in the desert sun, Moses in righteous anger, smashes to bits the tablets he has been carrying. So soon, so soon, Israel has broken the first and chief commandment against idolatry and in so doing has in effect transgressed them all. It is the first of a long record of broken promises which will scar Israel's and the world's history.

Back to the heights one final time goes Moses, there to fall on his face with a plea to God to take back these weak and confused people. No, says God, the people have betrayed their trust, now the blessing will be passed along Moses' own family line. At that, Moses, crying in protest, pounds the earth in prayer, until at length God relents and takes Israel back. The chosen nation has failed, yet in the midst of failure is being offered a second chance.

Can the experiment ever go right? Can one designated people become a blessing for all nations of the earth? For that to happen, each person, each family, each tribe will have to believe deeply in the dream and remain committed to its challenges.

Circle forward forty years; we are still with Israel in the desert. They are a more discerning and disciplined people now. The original escapees from Egypt have, all but a handful, gone to desert graves. A new generation has been born and bred tough as the terrain itself. These have been years of training, organizing, complaining, rebelling, finding reinstatement. Israel stands poised at last to cross the Jordan River and occupy the long promised land.

He is aged now, this man Moses. He has accomplished all kinds of things well, yet has made his share of mistakes, too. The immensity of the nation-building task has consumed the man. He longs to cross the Jordan and witness the plan's inauguration, yet that privilege will not be his, and this he well understands. With burning heart, he summons the elders of the Twelve Tribes one last time, to share his valedictory heart. He reviews the wonders God has worked on their behalf: their escape from Pharaoh's tyranny, the unimaginably safe crossing of the Red Sea, their preservation during the hardships of desert life. Often they have been chastened but never forsaken. Can the dream and the challenge carry over to a rising generation? The aged leader makes one final appeal:

> *Love the Lord your God with all your heart, with all your soul, and with all your might. That is the bedrock on which we build. And these words which I command you this day shall be upon your heart. Teach them diligently to your children; talk about them as you sit in your house or when you are out walking, when you go to bed at night, and when you get up in the morning. Bind them as strings on your fingers, reminders on your forehead. Carve them on the doorposts of your houses and the gates to your property.*

Is it possible? Can the dream of Sinai survive into the new generation and land? Can wisdom be handed down as legacy? Can children claim for themselves promises made to their parents? Must they bear the burden of sins committed by their parents? Is the entire concept of Covenant with God more than just a dream? Will it see fulfillment?

> *Make a promise — quite easily done.*
> *Keep a promise — ah, that is another matter.*
> *Make a promise — you are putting your character on the line.*
> *With time, you will reveal what kind of person you are. Since at best you are but human clay, you will need forgiveness to see you through.*

This retelling is based on Exodus chapter 24.

----

11. ATONEMENT-TOGETHER AGAIN

People living together are bound to hurt one another. Grievances are inevitable. When people do hurt one another, God's grace makes forgiveness possible. Day-in-day-out, at home, in the marketplace, or at the tent of worship, forgiveness is needed and asked for. Once each year, on Yom Kippur, Day of Atonement, forgiveness is sought for the whole nation.

Imagine Reb Tevye pulling his milk cart each morning door to door. We hear him praying to God about things close to his life. He prays with all his heart and soul. His prayers deal with his family, how he gets along with his wife, those men in the village who might make eligible husbands for his daughters, what it would be like to be a rich man; even the czar is not overlooked. His prayers are directed first upward toward God, then outward toward his fellow beings.

The Torah describes the web of relationships within which people live, move, and have their being. Sometimes they will get along well, at other times they will offend and hurt each other. People relate in five major areas:

1. *Sex and marriage.* Boundaries are prescribed for sexual relationships and conduct. Rules are established for marriage and divorce, duties laid out for parents toward children and children toward parents.

2. *The land and other real property.* Ownership rights are established with laws for passing property from one generation to the next. The soil is to be regarded as holy and cared for as a sacred trust.

3. *Commercial affairs.* Honest dealing is called for in the market place. The charging of interest (or usury) is prohibited. Courts are established for the settling of grievances.

4. *Matters of Public and Private Health.* Certain foods may be eaten and certain foods not. Rules define how food is to be prepared. We call these Kosher rules, the word signifying cleanness or purity.

5. *Worship.* Holy Places are designated, priestly lines established, rituals, seasons and their observance specified. Festivals will follow an annual cycle.

To safeguard these many relationships whether public or private, social contracts are drawn: husbands with wives, wives with husbands, parents with children, children with parents, next-door neighbor with next-door neighbor, employers with employees, employees with employers, citizens with magistrates, magistrates with citizens, and on and on. Sometimes such contracts are carefully written out and recorded, at other times they are spoken aloud in front of witnesses; most often they are simply taken for granted, ingrained within the society and culture.

Thus Moses and Joshua envision the nation completely under

the governance of God, with daily lives lived in observance of Torah rules. Call this theocracy — God is king above all, every citizen treats every other citizen decently, while a priestly class maintains peace and administers justice among God and people, neighbor and neighbor. By observing well these commandments and ordinances, the nation reaps blessing for itself and becomes light for the world.

However, human beings are clay; they will not always observe the commandments and ordinances. People will sin against God and sin against one another. What then? Can there be atonement, restoration, reconciliation? Can contracts once breached be re-negotiated? Can families and friendships once torn apart be woven together again? Can relationships grown cold become warm once more? Is forgiveness, indeed, always possible?

Yes, insists the Torah! For each sin committed, a corresponding sacrifice may be made. A list of offenses is matched by a parallel list of sacrifices designed to cancel out offenses committed. Fruits of the earth or the blood of animals will be offered to God to atone for laws broken. Some sacrifices will be offered by householders within the walls of their own home, others will be brought to places of worship for priests to consecrate by pouring them into the earth or burning them in fire.

And there is more! At Rosh Hashanah, New Year's time, the blast of the ram's horn will be heard in every village, announcing Yom Kippur, Day of Atonement! On this most solemn day of days, God will be asked to forgive the sins of every soul and set right every breach of law. People will examine their souls. At the great worship tent at Shiloh, all priests of the land will solemnly assemble. There in the holy place they will pour sacrificial blood onto the lid of the Ark of the Covenant ("the mercy seat"), praying for cleansing for themselves and for the people. A goat will be driven into the desert symbolically carrying away the nation's guilt -- a 'scapegoat' that is, sin-bearer for the nation, restorer of peace between God and people.

Thus all slates are wiped clean. Now let the New Year roll. Let the grand experiment once more surge forward!

Yes, there is forgiveness!

This retelling is based on the Book of Exodus, chapter 16 in particular.

----

12. TRUMPETS OF JUBILEE

Each fiftieth year the ram's horn will sound in every village, announcing the Year of Jubilee. Those who have fared poorly in financial matters, will find their debts wiped clean, their property restored. Tucked among the Bible's weightier scrolls, the tiny Story of Ruth gives a glimpse of the Torah's Jubilee laws in operation during lean times as well as prosperous.

In their little village of Bethlehem – the name means "House of Bread" — a farmer, Elimelech, and his wife, Naomi, have fallen on hard times. Famine has forced them to sell off their family farm. At this point they might place their two sons into indenture; instead they decide to pack up and move to the neighboring land of Moab, where work and food are still to be found. In Moab the two boys grow to manhood and marry Moabitish wives. Father Elimelech dies, and in quick succession both sons also die, leaving Naomi widowed and living with her two young, likewise widowed, daughters-in-law.

In such circumstance, Mosaic law calls for a younger, unmarried brother of the now deceased Elimelech to marry Naomi and produce offspring to inherit the family name and property. Naomi confides to her young daughters-in-law that she is too old to consider remarriage and babies, so let these young ladies stay on with their own people and remarry from among their own people, while she, Naomi, will travel back to Israel alone. One of the young women agrees to this proposal, but the other, Ruth, loves her mother-in-law too much to part company. She declares her affection in words which you likely have heard at some wedding celebration:

> *Entreat me not to leave you or return from following you. For where you go I will go, where you lodge I will lodge. Your people shall be my people and your God my God.*

Back in Bethlehem things take a turn for the better; farms and crops flourish once more. Elimelech's family farm, for years in the hands of third-parties, now carries market value pro-rated against years remaining until next Jubilee. Lacking funds for buying the land back, the two sojourning ladies must resort to gleaning in neighbors' fields. Gleaning, you recall, is the God-given right of the poor; rows of grain remain standing in the fields and fallen fruit is to be found lying exactly where it fell.

Naomi and Ruth make out well at gleaning. Yet the ever-ambitious Naomi is dreaming larger dreams for her attractive daughter-in-law. She sends Ruth to glean in the fields of Boaz, an eligible bachelor in town. Boaz, it so happens, is a relative of deceased Elimelech, albeit not a close relative. Enter romance between Boaz and Ruth — you might enjoy checking the somewhat spicy courtship details in the Bible account. Boaz determines he will marry Ruth. But this he cannot legally do, since there is a relative closer in line qualified to redeem both land and lady.

Love-driven, Boaz is not to be deterred. He searches out that closer living relative, the one eligible to make first offer toward redemption, and at the next town meeting formally asks this relative, does he wish to exercise his prior claim? "You understand, of course," Boaz adds, "the widow's daughter-in-law, Ruth, goes along with the property." The relative shakes his head sadly, "I might enjoy that, but I'm afraid my wife would object." They enjoy a laugh, then, technicalities satisfied, Boaz is free to redeem the land, wed the lovely Ruth, and with her live happily ever after.

But hold on! The end of the romance is not yet. Boaz and Ruth have but months to wait for the arrival of their first son and heir, Obed, a child whom Naomi pronounces the finest baby in all the land. This son will in due course inherit the Elimelech property. As years unfold he will also become grandfather to David of Bethlehem, of whom you must surely have heard, and of whom we shall hear more, directly.

And that, good reader, is how you build a country where there are no poor — at least back in those 'simpler' times. Call it justice, call it compassion, or call it any other name, it is forgiveness focused where forgiveness is also needed, the economic realm. Everyone must have a chance to earn a decent living.

When will humanity learn to use the resources of the earth so that everyone may plant and harvest the good gifts of God? When will our global planners consider the poor as equal in God's sight to the rich? There is a spiritual dimension to economics that dare not be overlooked.

This retelling is based on Exodus chapter 25 and the Book of Ruth.

----

13. THE PRINCE, THE POWER, THE PERIL

When public officials betray public trust, should they be forgiven? Does not betrayal of public trust place leaders beyond the possibility of redemption?

Somewhere in the Bible a writer pleads:

> *That prayers, intercessions and thanksgivings be made for kings and all in high positions, that we may lead a quiet and peaceable life, godly and respectful in every way.*

We are foolish, are we not, to expect that princes, presidents, and judges should be more righteous than we ourselves? Yet, that we do. Were we wiser, we might consider that the faults and failures of our leaders are little different from our own. True, their responsibilities are more conspicuous, their deeds and misdeeds viewed on a larger screen, but we are all responsible creatures and we all sometimes go wrong. Were we to offer more fervent prayers both for ourselves and for our leaders, then together we might be forgiven and allowed a much needed fresh start. Prayers for forgiveness would be good for our nation. They would certainly have been good for Israel when David was king.

As we pick up the story, the armies of Israel are engaged in battle on a distant front, while King David conducts affairs of state in Jerusalem. He can scarcely imagine the hurt and betrayal he is about to set in motion when from his palace roof he admires the beautiful Bathsheba bathing in her pool. Discreetly he inquiries and learns that the lady is already the wife of Uriah the Hittite, a junior officer in the army of Israel, currently on active duty with his troops in the distant battle zone.

For David temptation burns. People will scarcely deny the king his desires. Discreetly he invites the lady Bathsheba to his own chamber and there they bed. No one else need know. What business could that possibly be of the nation or of the people?

Weeks go by, and discreetly the lady conveys word to the king: "We are to have a child." Discreetly David sends word to Joab, his trusted field commander, "Put Uriah, the lady's husband, on orders for temporary leave back here in Jerusalem, I need him." When the young officer arrives, David inquires how things are going in the battle zone, then suggests that Uriah spend well-deserved days and nights with his wife at home. Now, should a child be born to Bathsheba, tongues need not wag, her husband is known to have been home on leave. However, Uriah, committed soldier that he is, declines the king's offer of home and wife while his men must bleed in battle. Instead he takes quarters for the night among the palace guard, and next morning is off again for the front.

So, the king's problem remains unresolved; moreover, time has been lost. Reluctantly he reaches for the ultimate solution. To his field commander another message is dispatched: "Set Uriah in the extreme forefront of the hardest fighting, then pull back, that he may be struck down." The instruction is received and carried out. Joab's next dispatch to the king reports cryptically, "Your servant Uriah the Hittite is among the dead."

David breathes easier now. He encourages his grieving aides to take news of battle losses in stride. "Buck up, war is hell; the sword claims now one, now another; just press this war effort all the harder." The king is free now to court the widow Bathsheba in plain sight, and soon adds the lady to his harem. Who's to know their secret, made all the more delightful since it is between just the two of them? True, there is Joab the commander, but Joab can be trusted to keep mum about the king's indiscretions; you see, the king well knows some of Joab's own.

One day as the king is conducting court, into the palace comes Nathan, a trusted adviser – the Billy Graham, one might say, of his day. He requests a private audience to discuss a troubling matter:

It seems that in a certain nearby village, a rich man and a poor man dwell side by side. The rich man owns extensive flocks of sheep, while the poor man owns — we should say, had owned — just one ewe lamb, his children's pet which shared their home and was fed at their table. When that rich man arranged a feast for his friends, he seized the poor man's lamb and served it as mutton for his guests. Hearing the prophet's report, David blazes with rage: "That man deserves to die! He must be prosecuted to the fullest extent of the law."

For a long moment Nathan looks silently at his king, then quietly declares,

You are the man. Thus says the Lord, I anointed you

king over Israel, delivered you out of the hand of Saul, gave you your master's wives into your bosom, gave you the House of Israel and of Judah; and if this were too little, I would add to you as much more. Why have you despised the word of the Lord to do what is evil in God's sight?"

David, his sin exposed, turns livid once more, this time blushing at his own guilt, "I have sinned against the Lord." Strange, is it not, how often we conceal our wrongdoings? Only when our misdeeds have been brought to light by others or by chance, do we say how sorry we are about them. Sorry, indeed, but for the people we have hurt or for the ignominy of our own failure?

Long nights follow during which the king's conscience will allow him no rest. He paces the floor, angry at himself. Then in an early hour he seizes his pen to let flow a torrent of confession. One day his words will find their way into the Bible and from there become the prayer of many another soul stricken by guilt and shame. These are David's words:

Have mercy on me, O God, according to your steadfast love; according to your abundant mercy blot out my transgression. Wash me thoroughly from my iniquity and cleanse me from my sin.

For I know my transgression and my sin constantly flashes before me. Against you, you only have I sinned and done that which is evil in your sight. Behold, you desire truth in the inner being, oh, teach me wisdom in my secret heart.

Create in me a clean heart, O God, and put a new and right spirit within me. Cast me not away from your presence and take not your Holy Spirit from me. Restore to me the joy of your salvation and up-hold me with a willing spirit.

For you do not delight in sacrifice. Were I to bring a burnt offering, you would not be moved. The sacrifice acceptable to God is a broken spirit, a broken and contrite heart, O God, you will not despise.

The king's proud heart has been laid wide open. Prophet Nathan has more to say — a two-fold message of forgiveness and of price still to be paid:

The Lord has put away your sin, you shall not die,

Forgiveness, indeed, yet sad times lie ahead for the king, for Bathsheba, and for the nation:

Nevertheless, because you have scorned the Lord, the child to be born to you shall die.

The prince . . . the power . . . the peril . . . the penitence . . . the pardon . . . the price.

Somewhere in the Bible a writer pleads that prayers, intercessions, and thanksgivings be made for kings and all in high positions, that we may lead a quiet and peaceable life, godly and respectful in every way. Were we to offer more fervent prayers both for ourselves and for our leaders, then together we might be forgiven and allowed a much needed fresh start.

This retelling is based on II Samuel chapter 11 and Psalm 51.

----

14. SONGS THAT BLESS THE SINGERS

The Psalms — the Bible's songs — speak often of for-
giveness, though not in narrative form. True, we have just
heard the story of David's sin and redemption, and do
find his song of confession included among the Bible's
150 psalms, yet such one-on-one linkage is rare. For the
most part, the Psalms are songs growing out of the people,
expressing hope, fear, discouragement, thanksgiving, plus
a whole range of emotions more. As we listen, we may
compose our own story — a shadow-story, if you will —
about common folks joining to sing "Songs that Bless the
Singers."

In the village of Shiloh, a long day's journey northward from
Jerusalem, lives a family of the tribe of Ephraim: the father
Seth, the mother Sarah, and their three little daughters, Abby,
Becky and Ruth. By day Seth tills his fields, then at sundown
returns home to enjoy the evening meal with his loved ones.
At the table he asks God's blessing on the food which Sarah
has prepared. Then, their supper finished, he takes down from
the high shelf his precious flute which is his delight to play.
His father taught him to play when he was still a boy; now he
has promised that he will teach their daughters to play as they

grow older.

He needs no parchment for words or notes, for he has long since learned these songs of Israel by heart from parents, teachers, cantors in the village, or from the Levite choirs that sing at festival times in the great tent of worship which stands in their own village and is a magnet for talented musicians of the land. He warms his lips with a few scales, then asks which song the children would like to sing. Each has her favorite, and as each begins to sing the others quickly join in.

At length the father says, "Let's learn a new song tonight, one about forgiving. Abby, tell us again what forgiving means." The oldest child, now a beaming five, replies, "It's when some-body hurts you and you say you still love them anyway." The father nods as he plays through the simple melody, then lays the flute on his lap to teach the girls these words:

> *Happy are those whose sins are forgiven, whose wrongs are pardoned, Happy is the one whom the Lord does not accuse of doing wrong and one who is free from all deceit.*

"Do you think we are forgiven people?" asks Seth. "Do you think our family is a favored one?" "Oh, yes," the daughters reply almost as one. Once more the father nods and sings:

> *When I did not confess my sins, I was worn out from crying all day long; My strength was completely drained as moisture is dried up by the summer heat.*

"When we've done something wrong, sometimes we choose to hide the wrong and not tell anybody, even God. Then we hurt inside and cry and find it hard to fall asleep at night. Then it is good to remember to pray to God once more – like this:

Then I confessed my sins to you, I did not conceal my
wrongdoings. I decided to confess them to you —and
you forgave all my sins.

"So God invites his people, every one, to pray and ask for forgiveness. That way we remember that God loves us very much and things will turn out right." Once more the father sings:

So all your loyal people should pray to you in times
of need, when a great flood of trouble comes rush
ing in. The Lord says, I will teach you the way you
should go. I will instruct you and advise you.

The father's eyes are closed now as he calls to mind the ancient farewell sayings of Moses: "These words shall be upon your hearts; teach them diligently to your children when you sit in your house or walk by the way, when you lie down and when you rise." The little girls have long since been yawning and nodding. "Bed time!" calls Sarah, "but sing one more, Papa!" So, one more time the melody on the flute, then the psalm they like best of all:

Bless the Lord, O my soul, and all that is within me,
bless God's holy name; Bless the Lord, O my soul,
and forget not all his benefits. The Lord is merciful
and gracious, slow to anger and abounding in stead
fast love. As a father pities his children, so the Lord
pities those who fear him.

Becky and little Ruth are already sound asleep while Abby struggles to keep her eyes open. The lamp on the table burns low. Seth and Sarah look into each other's eyes. Already they feel their years slipping too quickly away:

As for man, his days are as grass, as a flower of the

field so he flourishes, The wind passes over it and it is gone and its place knows it no more. But the steadfast love of the Lord is from everlasting to everlasting upon those who fear him, and his righteousness to children's children, to those who keep his covenant and remember to do his commandments. Bless the Lord, O my soul!

One by one the girls are carried safely to their beds. The flute is stored carefully on the shelf. The lamp on the table is snuffed.

Behold, he who keeps Israel will neither slumber nor sleep.

This imagined story includes lines from Psalms 32, 103 and 121.

----

15. A KING WHO FED HIS ENEMIES

When enemies invade your land, should you feed them and wish them well? Would you not do better to annihilate them, first chance you get?

Machiavelli put it bluntly: if a king cannot deal properly with his enemies, the people will somehow find themselves a new ruler who can. History bears that out. By dealing properly with enemies, Machiavelli meant: neutralize them by peaceful means if possible, and if that does not work, then attack, starve, destroy. The duty of a king is to protect his people from enemies at all costs; failing that, he forfeits his right to rule. Fair enough.

To come upon the story of a king who, when he has his enemies trapped, instead of attacking, starving, and destroying them, invites them to a hearty thanksgiving dinner and sends them home to their families, leaves us astonished. Especially surprising it is to discover this story among the annals of the rulers of the Divided Kingdoms of Israel, since almost without exception, the kings of this era, both North and South, are insecure monarchs, remembered principally for their cunning, cruelty, and vindictiveness. For most of these kings, the very thought of inviting enemies to a feast would appear utter nonsense.

So listen:

Syria is neighbor and long-standing archrival to Israel's Northern Kingdom. During drawn-out border struggles between these two adjoining states, the King of Syria senses a moment of advantage. He dispatches raiding parties to harass Israel's border regions and weaken its defenses. His efforts are consistently thwarted because, so his spies inform him, the prophet Elisha is counseling the Israelite king. To deal with this, the Syrian king sends crack mounted troops to surround Elisha's house and take him prisoner. Elisha's servant-boy, seeing Syrian horsemen, charioteers, and foot-soldiers closing in on all sides, cries out in terror to his master. But Elisha asks God to sharpen the eyes of the young man, who now can see a divine firewall of angels fending off the Syrian troops.

For their part, the Syrian invaders have by now become lost, and are heading directly toward the army of the Israelite king, who lies poised to strike. Well aware of his advantage, the king shouts to his prophet,

> *Now, Father Elisha? Shall we begin the slaughter now?*

To which Elisha shouts back,

> *For God's sake, man, no! Would you execute prisoners of war? Do not harm a single one. Feed these hungry soldiers and send them back to their homes!*

Whereupon the king summons not executioners but cooks and waiters. He serves the Syrian troops what is described as 'a mighty feast.' When that sumptuous meal is concluded, he bids them Godspeed and sends them on their way, well fed and healthy, back to their units and families.

Comes now the bottom line of the story:

> And the Syrians conducted no more raids into the land of Israel.

Calories and compassion have carried the day. The sword has been sheathed — for at least one full generation.

Wars are fought, we have already observed, to further national interests, advance frontiers, lay claim to resources, control trade routes. Economic sanctions are imposed to weaken the enemy's will to resist. Time-honored strategy calls for starving the foe into submission so he will be forced to yield on the victor's terms.

What if nations were given the vision of Elisha, and would adopt a strategy of economic cooperation? What if instead of imposing sanctions to deprive an enemy of resources, a feast of incentive could be served in the form of food, clothing, shelter, education, medical care? Could such a course be justified as national policy, or must it remain forever an impractical dream?

At the close of World War II, when Germany and her Axis allies lay broken in the rubble of defeat, there were counselors who advocated grinding the Axis powers into the dust of perpetual poverty, the way Rome once pounded Carthage into the African sands, no more to rise. Wiser heads carried the day, and the Marshall Plan instead supplied the Axis nations with wherewithal to re-build their shattered economies. That was a rare moment in the annals of human relations.

Now, carry that success story one step beyond. What if we were not to wait until the enemy lies exhausted in rubble? What if nations were to pursue a policy of preemptive peace — study each other's basic needs, then put forth the equivalent of war's effort to help the others satisfy those needs?

What if we were to divert dollars now devoted to proliferating weapons of defense to helping those we consider enemy build roads, houses, clinics, hospitals, schools, and libraries for their people, firewalls of cooperation instead of the firebolts of destruction? Would Machiavelli call that dealing properly with one's enemies? I think he would; after all, Machiavelli was a very practical man.

In the Bible's Book of Proverbs a sage writer offers counsel that rulers and people alike would do well to ponder:

> *If your enemy is hungry, give him food, if he is thirsty, give him drink. That is the way to heap burning coals on his head.*

This retelling is based on II Kings chapter 6 and Proverbs chapter 25.

----

16. A TONGUE TOUCHED BY FIRE

Prophets there were in those days – sages of rare insight and courage who in times of crisis counseled kings and commoners – then, contemplating times and lands beyond, helped instruct nations still to be. If that sounds noble, be warned, no prophet ever found his calling an easy one.

In Jerusalem, a young man climbs the long staircase leading to Solomon's Temple. Judging by the simple clothes he wears, you might hardly suspect that he is kin to the royal family of Judah. The protocols and pleasures of the palace offer this young man little satisfaction: he prefers the company of scholars in the holy place. The young man's name is Isaiah — "Salvation is of God" — a name which he and others take seriously.

The sun has barely melted the morning haze as he pauses for prayer before the great sacrificial altar at the temple entrance. Smoke has begun to ascend from the altar, silently raising thanks to God who has protected the land during the night watches. A small choir chants near the steps to the Holiest Place. Though he may not enter that Holiest Place, the young man's thoughts penetrate its walls. There, enveloped in darkness, rests the Ark of the Covenant containing the tablets with the words of the Torah, documenting Israel's ancient call and destiny. The young man's heart is heavy as he laments the present sad state of morals among his countrymen. Israel, he fears, is spiritually sick, head to toe; surely judgment cannot be long in arriving.

As Isaiah rises from his knees, the pavement beneath him begins to buckle and sway. The walls of the temple quiver as smoke issues from between its massive building blocks. Through eyes of ecstasy, Isaiah envisions God seated on a heavenly throne, attended by angelic courtiers.

The young man protests aloud his own sinfulness,

> *I have no right to stand in the presence of God, I am a man of unclean lips, living among people of unclean lips!*

Whereupon an angel with seraphic tongs lifts a burning coal from the altar of sacrifice and touches it to the lips of the youth, declaring,

> *Your guilt is taken away and your sin forgiven!*

Now the voice of God inquires,

> *Whom shall we send? Who will go for us?*

In ecstatic fervor Isaiah cries out,

> *I will go! Send me!*

Called to be prophet, this young man can scarcely imagine

what momentous challenges lie in store. Yet he is not naïve; the life of a prophet, he knows, will be anything but easy. The voice of God goes on

> *You will speak, but people will not listen. The land*
> *will be forsaken and the people carried into exile.*

Such a dire message to deliver, such a gloomy commission to fulfill! Who would choose to be prophet unless driven by an irresistible inner urge? Isaiah is driven by such zeal. He will indeed become God's messenger. Moreover, his message will not be one of judgment alone; does not his very name, Isaiah, signify salvation? Ultimately his message is to be one of redemption:

> *Come now, let us reason together, says the Lord;*
> *though your sins be like scarlet, they shall be white*
> *as snow; though they be red like crimson, they shall*
> *become like wool. If you are willing and obedient,*
> *you shall eat the good of the land, but if you refuse*
> *and rebel, you shall be devoured by the sword.*

Isaiah's term of service will stretch across the reigns of four successive Judean kings – Uzziah, Jotham, Ahaz and Hezekiah. He will advise each of these Judean monarchs in turn, as tensions steadily worsen between their own kingdom, Judah, and Israel, their estranged sister kingdom to the north.

During Ahaz' reign in Judah (the South), the sister Northern Kingdom will attempt the unthinkable — form an alliance with neighboring Syria to wipe the southern sister-state clean off the map. Since the combined might of those two northern neighbors appears irresistible, Isaiah's king quakes from fear. Isaiah counsels:

> *Calm your trembling heart, the Alliance is doomed*

to fail.

The Lord will give you a sign. A young woman will conceive and bear a son and will call his name Immanuel — "God with us." Before the child is grown, the Northern Kingdom and her ally Syria will cease to be inhabited. They will be wiped clean off the map.

These words of the prophet will find an enduring place in the Judean soul, not only now, but in times to come. "Immanuel, God with us," is the motto of the land, a perpetual plea for divine deliverance.

Thundering out of the distant East, intent on challenging Egypt for control of the western world, now roll the mighty armies of Assyria. Before them, the overmatched allied forces of Syria and Israel scatter like straw in the wind. The entire ten northern tribes of Israel are led away captive toward eastern lands, there to meet an unknown fate. 'Ten Lost Tribes of the House of Israel' are absorbed into the amalgam of Asiatic genealogy.

Relentlessly toward the gates of Jerusalem the 'unstoppable' forces of Assyria continue to roll. Poet George Gordon Byron describes the inevitability of their intent:

> *The Assyrian came down like the wolf on the fold,*
> *And his cohorts were gleaming in purple and gold;*
> *And the sheen of their spears was like stars on the sea,*
> *When the blue wave rolls nightly on deep Galilee.**

On the southern throne presently sits the untried Prince Hezekiah. The youth trembles to watch the Assyrians throw up siege-works against the walls of his capital. "Surrender or die," comes their taunt. We offer you 2000 horses, provided you can muster 2000 live troops to put on them." Hezekiah trembles, but Isaiah braces him, "You must not give up!"

From the Assyrian's commander comes a final note of warning: "Do not trust that God of yours. If the gods of the other nations could not save them, what makes you think your God can save you? Resist and your people will perish, surrender and they will be allowed to live in peace." In anguish, Hezekiah seizes the parchment, rushes with it to the temple of God, to spread before the altar. Perhaps for the sake of God's people, it is his duty to surrender. But Isaiah will not relent; once more the prophet insists,

> *Have no fear, the Lord has his own ultimatum for*
> *that arrogant Assyrian: I will put my hook in your*
> *nose and my bit in your mouth and turn you back on*
> *the road by which you came.*

That night, plague rages through the Assyrian camp, claiming the lives of no fewer than 185,000 of Sennacherib's seasoned warriors. At roll-call next morning, survivors receive their orders: "Abandon camp, strike for home." The poet describes the scene:

> *Like the leaves of the forest when summer is green*
> *That host with their banners at sunset were seen;*
> *Like the leaves of the forest when autumn has blown*
> *The host on the morrow lay withered and strown.*

> *For the angel of death spread his wings on the blast,*
> *And breathed in the face of the foe as he passed;*
> *And the eyes of the sleepers waxed deadly and chill,*
> *And their hearts but once heaved and forever grew still.*

> *And the widows of Ashur are loud in their wail,*
> *And the idols are broke in the temple of Baal;*

And the might of the Gentile, unsmote by the sword
Hath melted like snow in the glance of the Lord. *

For the moment, the Assyrian juggernaut has been halted, yet the threat from the East is by no means at an end. Soon a new empire, Babylon, having overthrown the diminished might of Assyria, will send fresh armies westward, once more to challenge Egypt for world supremacy. Once again Jerusalem, lying in the path of conquest, will find itself besieged. This time resistance fails. The capital city, including its magnificent temple, goes up in flames. The bulk of the Judean populace, except for a few infirm and poor, are driven in chains toward the banks of the Tigris.

Even now, aging Isaiah's confidence does not falter. He anticipates the day when Babylon, too, will be overthrown and Jerusalem once more lifted as a beacon of hope for the world. Once more a king will occupy the throne, a green shoot springing from the stump of David's truncated dynasty:

> *For to us a child is born, to us a son is given; and the*
> *government shall be upon his shoulder. His name will*
> *be called Wonderful Counselor, Mighty God, Ever-*
> *lasting Father, Prince of Peace. Of the increase of*
> *his government and of peace there will be no end,*
> *upon the throne of David and over his kingdom to*
> *establish it and to uphold it with justice and with*
> *righteousness from this time forth and for evermore.*
> *The zeal of the Lord of hosts will do this.*

Israel will yet become light to the nations. The dream will live, the way toward peace remain open. To those who yearn for the Righteousness Kingdom, the prophecy rings clear:

> *Come, let us go to the house of the God of Jacob,*

that he may teach us his ways and that we may walk in his paths. For out of Zion shall go forth the law and the word of the Lord from Jerusalem. He shall judge between the nations and shall decide for many peoples. They shall beat their swords into plowshares and their spears into pruning hooks; nation shall not lift up sword against nation, neither shall they learn war any more.

The prophet, now full of years, has more than lived up to his name. His words will not cease to strike hope and healing to the hearts of Judea's exiles and many a generation beyond:

Isaiah — 'Salvation is of God!'

This retelling draws selectively on the Writings of Isaiah chapters 1-39.
* "The Destruction of Sennacharib"

----

17. THE SONG A SERVANT SANG

*In Babylon, far removed from their ravaged homeland, the
Exiles of Judah mourn, then thrill to the rallying cry of
a new Isaiah.*

Strange is it not, how we take for granted good things while
we have them, only to miss them desperately once they are
taken away. Once the captives of Judah have been resettled a
thousand miles from home, they begin to appreciate blessings
which in their own country they often dismissed with a shrug.
Now they long for sight of the Temple which once graced Zi-
on's summit but is no more: the smoke rising from its altar, the
sound of choirs echoing from its courtyards. Scattered now in
ghettos and settlements, they long to hear again the words of
the Torah and the pleadings of the prophets.

"Sing for us your Hebrew songs," their Babylonian captors
taunt. But the words of the Psalms stick in the exiles' throats,
even as their harps hang unstrung on the willows beside the
waterways.

Still, God has not forgotten his people, nor have the people totally forgotten God. Even now their scholars are searching ancient scrolls, laboring to set in order the words of Moses and more contemporary prophets. By lamplight in a thousand homes, devout Seths and Sarahs still teach their children the Ten Commandments and the beloved Psalms. Synagogue schools draw eager teachers and students, while the Sabbath is observed devoutly in many a home.

Listen, can you hear the sound of harps being tuned once more, aging voices humming ancient melodies for younger ears to catch and repeat, young fingers setting ancient psalms to contemporary chords?

And, say, have you heard the young prophet, that new and charismatic Isaiah, moving camp to camp, stirring faithful souls with promises that bespeak a better day?

> *Israel will be born again! Get ready for the journey back home! God is laying before us a new and better day! Prepare for God a roadway in your hearts!*

> *Comfort, comfort my people, says your God! Speak tenderly to Jerusalem and cry to her that her warfare is ended, her iniquity pardoned, that she has received from the Lord's hand double for all her sins!*

God, who long ago rescued his people from Egyptian bondage, led them dry-shod through the waters of the Red Sea, and opened before them a land of milk and honey, will set his people free once more. Sins of the past will be forgiven, hearts will be cleansed by Heaven's abundant grace:

> *I am he who blots out your transgressions. For my own sake, I will not remember your sins.*

Breaking news! The might of Babylon is itself under siege. Cyrus, charismatic commander of Persian forces is marching his phalanxes northward toward Babylon, laying waste to fortress after fortress along the Babylonian chain of defenses. Now the capital itself falls before his relentless drive. To the young Isaiah, this Persian general is a chosen instrument of God – a messiah, savior, deliverer. Cyrus will liberate God's people. From house to house the prophet's words are buzzed:

> *The ransomed of the Lord shall return and come to*
> *Zion with singing!*

Now Cyrus has claimed the emperor's crown. Quickly he decrees that peoples once forcibly resettled by Babylon be given free passage to return to their homelands. Israel is free to go home! Again the young prophet's words fly through the camps: "Prepare for departure! Gird yourselves for the rigors of the long trip home. God is laying before us a task that will stretch our vision and test our commitment:

> *I will give you as a light to the nations, that my sal-*
> *vation may reach to the end of the earth. Nations*
> *shall come to your light and kings to the brightness*
> *of your rising. Lift your eyes and see, they all gather*
> *together, they come to you.*

> *My house shall be called a house of prayer for all*
> *people; thus says the Lord God who gathers the out-*
> *casts of Israel. I will gather others besides those al-*
> *ready gathered.*

And still more! Beneath this exuberant refrain of jubilant homecoming runs a somber counter-melody, a haunting recitative:

Behold my servant whom I uphold! He was despised and rejected by men, a man of sorrows and acquainted with grief; and as one from whom men hide their faces he was despised and we esteemed him not.

Surely he has borne our griefs and carried our sorrows, Yet we esteemed him stricken, smitten by God and afflicted. But he was wounded for our transgressions, he was bruised for our iniquities;. upon him was the chastisement that made us whole and with his stripes we are healed.

Israel, my servant, Jacob whom I have chosen, the offspring of Abraham, my friend, you whom I took from the ends of the earth, and called from its farthest corners – I say to you, you are my servant, I have chosen you and will not cast you off.

Chosen to be a servant? Selected by God to suffer? Will these exiles, eagerly packing for the long journey to the homeland, now see themselves cast in the role of servant? Will they consider themselves expendable for a world in need, committed to bear as their own the griefs and sorrows of other peoples?

One day a young preacher from Nazareth, who would be king, steeped in the spirit of young Isaiah, will shape his career and that of his followers to the beat of that counter-melody and declare: "The Son of Man came not to be served but to serve and to give his life a ransom for many. Would you be great, then to others become servant; would you be chief, then to others become slave."

Who would rally to a battle-cry and banner such as that?

This retelling is based on II Chronicles chapter 36 and the later chapters of the collected writings of Isaiah.

----

18. JONAH, RELUCTANT PROPHET

*Israel, now restored to its homeland, must ask how far its
spiritual responsibility extends. Ought God's mercy be of-
fered to nations that have attempted to wipe out our own?*

Jonah's assignment is anything but simple; being swallowed by
a 'whale' will not be that man's biggest claim to fame. Jonah is
a prophet, a reluctant prophet, faced with an 'impossible' task.
When he realizes the job God has planned for him, he does
not, like Isaiah, shout, "Here I am, Lord, send me!" Instead,
he flees post-haste in the opposite direction, simply runs away.
The reason he runs away is his conviction that God is far more
forgiving than God has any right to be. Here is a drama that
pits God's mercy against human reluctance to give and forgive.

Jonah, son of Amittai, hears a call from God:

> *Go at once to Ninevah, that great city, and cry out
> against it, for their wickedness has come up before me.*

Ninevah!!! Keep in mind, if you will, Ninevah is the capital of Assyria, and Assyria is the nation that decimated Israel's Northern tribes, wiping them as a people off the scroll of history. Say Ninevah, you are saying holocaust. How can the Jews, now in the flush of renewed patriotism and pride, possibly pray for Ninevah's redemption? Yet it is precisely to Ninevah that Jonah is being sent by God to put forward the offer of repentance.

Jonah at once books passage on a ship, not a vessel headed east, mind you, but a freighter headed west, as far west as ships dare sail – Gibraltar, drop-off edge of the world. And will you blame the man for trying to evade an assignment that violates his own deep conviction? If God sends you on an 'impossible' mission, why not move out of God's range? If God inquires, "Can you hear me now?" why not simply refuse to answer? This is Jonah's way of responding to his 'impossible' mission. God will certainly not keep track of him at the very edge of civilization.

On the Mediterranean a mighty storm blows up. The sailors on Jonah's ship struggle hopelessly against the fury of the elements. They pray to their gods to deliver them, then shake the sleeping Jonah awake, demanding that he also pray to his God; every desperate prayer will help. But Jonah is not about to attempt contact with God from whom he is running away. To the captain he confesses his miserable situation and suggests that they simply throw him overboard in hope of calming the storm. With prayers to their gods for Jonah's soul, the sailors pick up and hurl the pathetic runaway into the sea.

To be sure, God was not beyond calling range after all. Enter now Leviathan, giant sea monster, to swallow the gasping Jonah at a single gulp. Alive inside the ichthyological marvel, the reluctant prophet spends three wretched days and nights reduced at last to prayer, both eloquent and fervent. Now he is willing to obey; he will do as he has been told. Whereupon Leviathan belches the prophet safely out onto dry land.

The call is heard a second time, a re-statement of the original 'impossible' mission: "Go to Ninevah, preach repentance!" This time the chastened prophet reluctantly turns his face eastward toward Ninevah. Once there, he walks the streets, clanging his bell, and crying: "Forty days and Ninevah will be overthrown! Forty days and Ninevah is slated to perish!"

Response to his cry is nothing less than astonishing, an overwhelming response such as no prophet within Israel's own borders has ever come near to experiencing. The people of Ninevah, to the very last soul, heed Jonah's warning and turn to fasting and repentance. From palace to hovel, they dress in the sackcloth of contrition. Even the king enters the ash-pit to declare:

> *We hereby renounce violence. Who knows, God may yet relent and turn from his fierce anger so that we do not perish.*

With that, God does indeed change the divine mind! God spares wicked Ninevah, that Third Reich of antiquity, and gives the nation a new chance.

Jonah is deeply resentful. Disgusted at God's change of heart, he sees himself as utterly humiliated. He lashes at God,

> *I told you so! I knew you would change your mind, leaving me to look like a stupid fool. That's the way you always act, and that, if you must know, is exactly why I tried to run out of your range in the first place. I knew you are a gracious God and merciful,*

slow to anger, and abounding in steadfast love and ready to relent. So all right, now you have done your divine thing. Kindly let me die.

Thirty-eight, thirty-nine, forty — the days pass and Ninevah's time of judgment is at hand. Jonah, still very much alive, has climbed the river bluff, taking refuge from the broiling sun under the shade of a castor-bean plant which has sprung up overnight. His cool, however, is short-lived, as a worm promptly invades the plant causing it to shrivel. Sweltering once more and in abject misery, Jonah pleads once more that God will let him die. But the voice of God is heard pressing the ultimate question:

> *You are so concerned about that bush for which you performed no labor. It came into being overnight and now has perished just as quickly. Should I not be concerned about Ninevah, that great city in which there are a multitude of souls who have never learned right from wrong? Should they not be offered another chance?*

On that unnerving note the curtain falls on our brief scan of the Hebrew portion of the Bible. Together with the restored nation, we are left with troubling questions:

> *Should we pray for enemies and wish them well? Would it not make more sense to pray that God would eliminate those who cause us harm, wipe them out entirely? If we ourselves are forbidden to take revenge, certainly the Almighty Lord can ac-*

complish revenge for us. Does God's mercy somehow supersede our notion of what is acceptable?

Does God actually change the divine mind when souls repent and plead for forgiveness? When it appears that God relents even as Ninevah repents, could it be that the Spirit has expanded our understanding of God and of divine grace?

This retelling is based on the books of Ezra and Jonah.

THE INN:
Lost on Long Loop Trail

I was certain that I had headed toward Short Loop Trail, out back of the Inn where the woods begin. "Just a quick walk to clear my brain before lunch," was the way I had phrased it to Abby. Mistakenly, I had started out on Long Loop which is four times the distance. By the time I realized my mistake and headed back, lunch had already been cleared away. As for my brain, it still desperately needed clearing; in fact, it was becoming more and more mixed up.

Henri and his stories had actually grabbed me at first. His old-world manner of speaking — French accent, oui, and those curious Asian and African expressions sprinkled in. He had announced that his stories would be about Israel the Nation, and that was true. But he was hardly underway when he remarked, "I see Israel as a family of families learning to live together. That is one way of looking at any nation – a family of families working to make things go for the good of everybody."

So, here we were talking family again. And talking family has become my rogue wave, making me face up to what I would rather forget.

Henri had dropped snatches about his own family. His parents had been connected to the French Consular service, which meant they had moved frequently with him and his sister from one former French colony to another — first to Lebanon, then Vietnam, from there to Madagascar, and finally to Algeria. He had grown up observing how some customs were much the same among those various peoples and cultures, but in other ways radically different.

People are people, whatever their tribal origins and customs. They all need to eat, put a roof over heads, get help when they fall sick, educate their children as best they can. To that end each nation develops its set of laws, its own Torah, so to speak, allowing families to live and work together: specific laws about sex and marriage, about land ownership, commercial dealings, health matters. People draw up social contracts with one another, husbands with wives, wives with husbands, employers with workers, on and on. These basic contracts, written or unwritten, make people responsible to each other and for each other. Somehow, that basic web of kinship and responsibility remains constant, whatever the culture -- that great, big, intricate web that ties into so many other webs.

The major difference among cultures is observable in the way the various peoples link together their laws and their beliefs. Israel's laws specifically link every human relationship and endeavor to the Creator God. Land, food, children, are considered as held in trust, each family and individual being accountable to God and to every other family and individual. Love God and love neighbor are twin pillars supporting Israel's social structure. Responsibility extends beyond self.

Henri repeatedly referred back to David's tearing of webs during his affair with Bathsheba. David had taken on huge responsibility as king, then messed up, and everyone in the nation had been forced to pay a price for his messing up. When David finally admitted his wrongdoing, he did acknowledge his sin against God: "Against you, you alone have I sinned and done this evil in your sight."

Which was, of course, true to the extent that he did own up — God was Lord, and David had sinned first and foremost against God. But on the corresponding neighbor side, David had grievously hurt the many people who depended on him. He had sinned against Uriah, the army captain, whose death he plotted to cover up the royal scandal. Sinned against Joab, commander-in-chief, whom he ordered to put in motion the death-plot. Sinned against his own palace advisers, to whom he lied in the name of national security. Sinned against his new wife Bathsheba, who would carry to full term a baby whom she would nurse for but a week, then carry to the grave. Sinned against the whole populace of Israel, whose affairs he had slighted while looking to his own indulgence. Right and left David had torn to shreds his webs of responsibility.

And with that kind of talk Henri set my rogue wave crashing over me again. When Allison and I had stood at the altar and promised to be faithful to each other "til death us do part," we had made promises to more than just each other and God. We had in effect also made promises to Allison's parents who had dreamed of a long, happy marriage for their daughter and possible grandchildren. Promises to our many friends who had adjusted their lives to see us as husband and wife. Promises to the church at whose altar we stood. Promises to Jamie and Julie as yet unborn, who would want father and mother to be by their side during their developing years. Promises to the community which would hear me say to two different spouses: "Til death us do part." And I had failed. I had torn my webs, I had hurt people, and Henri was skewering my conscience by reminding me of it.

I tell you, friend, this whole place is driving me batty. Who does that guy Henri think he is? By now, Abby probably questions my ability to make her a good husband. Why else does she look at me so strangely? I love you Abby, and nobody is going to interfere — not Henri, not anybody!

Lisa is due to talk next, that girl from the U of Montana — "dear Lisa", Levi Matthew insists on calling her. All right, dear Lisa, maybe you have something to say that will straighten me out.

BOOK THREE

KINGDOM

19. SPLASH AT THE JORDAN

We begin our scan of the New Testament with its stories of Jesus of Nazareth and his close followers. Here, at the outset, come four gospels – the word means "Good News" – under the titles "Matthew," "Mark," "Luke," and "John." Each opens with the appearance of a spellbinding preacher, John the Baptizer, who blazes across the Judean countryside proclaiming: "God's Kingdom is about to happen! Repent and be baptized for the forgiveness of sins!"

Along the streets of Jerusalem shopkeepers are closing their shutters. In homes men and women shake out musty backpacks, loading them with food and camp supplies enough for a week. Through the city runs a buzz: "John is baptizing at the River Jordan and we must go hear him!" By the time hikers complete their steep descent into the Jordan Valley, the banks along the river have already blossomed with a thousand multicolored tents. This is the biggest camp-meeting they have ever witnessed, and rumor has it, "John is announcing a new Kingdom. God is about to intervene in history on behalf of Israel. Rome, hated overlord and occupier in our land, will soon be driven out!"

Campers draw in their breath as they catch first sight of John standing on a rocky knoll beside the river, his face etched against the rays of the sun. A charge runs through the new arrivals — it is true, this man does look like Elijah, prophet of old, dressed as he is in a tunic of camel's skin, his red beard and waist-long locks gleaming in the morning light.

Presently the man extends his arms, holding them aloft until, section by section, the hubbub of the throng subsides. Then his voice booms loud and clear across the valley, reaching up to the tents farthest atop the hill:

> *Sons and daughters of Israel, the Kingdom of God*
> *is about to happen and we must be ready for it! Turn*
> *your hearts to God, and God will forgive us our*
> *wrongs, then come among us to accomplish wonders.*
> *Once more we'll know we are God's chosen people.*
> *Come, be washed, become clean inside and out!*

Down from his rocky pulpit into the river the preacher springs, the crowd surging in after him, pushing to be near, as he scoops great armfuls of water over them, shouting,

> *I wash you for the forgiveness of sins in the name*
> *of the Lord God of Israel, and in expectation of the*
> *Kingdom soon to come!*

Those already baptized scramble up the river-banks, while others leap into the shallows. A cantor begins words of an ancient psalm and soon the crowd has joined the singing. Late into the afternoon the preaching and baptizing continue.

Next morning long before dawn, storm clouds blow swiftly into the valley. People scurry in the darkness to secure their tent-ropes. Lightning flashes and thunder booms along the valley with earsplitting fury. Daylight refuses to break and rain descends in sheets, flushing down the slippery banks to swell the river. In his tent-door stands John surveying the storm, contemplating calling off preaching for the day.

Suddenly out of the darkness emerges the figure of a man running, splashing, shouting as he nears, "John, Cousin, Friend! This is the Day of the Lord!" John trembles as his heart tells him he is seeing one unlike others. Could this possibly be God's Chosen One, Israel's awaited Messiah? The man cries:

Baptize me, John!

Hold on, friend, should not you be baptizing me?

Together! Together we will launch God's righteous plan!

John relents. Then slipping, half sliding down the bank, the two descend to water's edge and splash on out into the swollen, charging current. The man is plunged beneath the rushing water as John shouts against a great clap of thunder:

Jesus of Nazareth, I baptize you in the name of the Lord God of Israel and the coming, righteous Kingdom!

The heavy clouds roll southward through the valley, the booming thunder slackens as light of day struggles through. Rain continues to pelt down as the two men, bracing their feet against the current's force, embrace and laugh in holy ecstasy. John's voice is heard rising in a psalm well-known to the campers:

O give thanks to the Lord who is good, whose steadfast love endures for ever! This is the day which the Lord has made, let us rejoice and be glad in it!

Save us we beseech thee, O Lord! Hosanna, hosanna!
O Lord, we beseech thee, grant success!

With that, the storm which moved swiftly in, as swiftly moves southward through the Great Rift Valley. A fresh wind sweeps from the north scattering the last of the overcast. The sun breaks through, warm and radiant, its rays glancing off the river's churning surface. A canopy of blue stretches wide, and from it descends a single white dove to alight on the shoulder of the Nazarene — this for John a sign long awaited. Out of the thunder rolling in the distance he hears a voice echoing words of an ancient coronation psalm:

This is my Son, my Beloved; with him I am well pleased!

The camp stirs to life. People struggle to dry out soggy tents and coax reluctant fires to cook their morning meal. The refrain of John's psalm is heard tent to tent, until soon from all sides throughout the camp the song resounds:

This is the day which the Lord has made!
Save us, we cry, O, Lord!
Hosanna, hosanna!
O Lord, grant success!"

The man called Yeshua — Jesus — has, like his ancient namesake Joshua, stepped boldly into the Jordan to usher in God' s New Kingdom. Now, as suddenly as he appeared out of the darkness, he is gone again, last seen following the retreating storm southward through the Great Rift Valley toward the southern desert.

Once more John mounts his great boulder-pulpit at river's edge. This time the crowd is already hushed and waiting:

People of Israel, turn your hearts to God, that God

*may forgive our nation its sins and walk once more
among us to work mighty deeds!*

*Some of you, I have no doubt, own two coats; well,
give one to some poor soul who has no coat at all.
Some of you, I am sure, have enough to eat and
more; consider then what it's like to be starving —
open a place for the hungry at your table. You sol-
diers, quit grumbling about your pay, and don't take
advantage of the very people you are supposed to be
protecting.*

Some in the crowd squirm uneasily at John's words. Others ap-
plaud, shouting, "Right on, preacher!" John holds every listener:

*Did you see that man I baptized early this morning?
I am not worthy to stoop down and tie his sandal
strings. Here I am washing you with water; that man
is about to wash you with the very Spirit of God!*

John's words hit their mark. Tents are folded and camp gear
repacked. Back in Jerusalem, customers wait for shop-shutters
to be reopened and wares set out once more. On Jordan's banks
new arrivals stream into camp, scrambling to claim campsites
just vacated. The new arrivals draw in their breath as they
catch first sight of that preacher-man, auburn hair flashing in
the day's early sun.

It is true, he does look like Elijah!

This retelling is based Mark chapter 1, Matthew chapter 3 and Luke chapter 3.

----

20. MAP FOR A KINGDOM

In a month-long fast in the Dead Sea desert, Jesus of Nazareth struggles to chart the course of his career.

The storm has blown itself out, yet the wind of the Spirit urges forward the Man from Nazareth. Half walking, half running, he pushes southward under clear skies. Now he enters a forbidding wasteland where towering bare cliffs rise above a great salt lake, that lake into which Jordan's waters pour but from which they find no exit, the sea named Dead. Here life in even its barest forms must cower to survive. No blade of grass welcomes him, only boulders blasted clear of all trace of soil by the winds of centuries. Above him loom gigantic crags, while underfoot twisting wadis still glisten from the recent storm. Here Jesus of Nazareth will search his soul to determine the mission to which God is calling him. Like Jacob at the Stream Jabbok, he will wrestle in prayer until an answer be found.

He senses in his soul powers implanted by heaven. Could he not turn the very stones at his feet into bread to satisfy his own present hunger, and more significantly, to nourish the wasting bodies of his many countrymen forced to live at the brink of starvation? Might not this, in fact, be the very purpose of his baptism — to bring to reality Moses' dream of a nation where injustice, hunger, and poverty are no longer known, where each family is free to till its acre and prune its orchard in peace and security?

He recalls how Moses in the Sinai barrenness pleaded earnestly to God for food to revive the exhausted ex-slaves. Moses had witnessed heaven's answer, manna, bread from heaven, and quail incredibly blown into the leafless wilderness. Yet the people, once fed, had only murmured the more, always demanding, demanding until Moses, losing patience, had been driven to shout: "God humbled you and allowed you to go hungry that he might make you realize that mankind does not live by bread alone but by every word that proceeds from the mouth of God." Besides, has it not been all too plain that nations once well-fed and grown fat with economic gain easily wander far from God's purposes?

With a defiant shout Jesus rebukes the unseen Tempter:

> *Not by bread alone, but by every word out of the mouth of God!*

Empty canyons echo back his cry:

> *Every word from God. . . from God."*

His search must go on, his fast by no means at an end.

If indeed he is called to lead Israel into the New Kingdom, then he must be recognized by people and rulers alike as God's prophet and Christ. Far to the east, glistening in the morning sun, his eye catches the gleam of Jerusalem's temple dome. Had not Malachi, last great prophet before John, foretold that God would come suddenly to his temple? Would not a dramatic leap from the topmost pinnacle down into the crowd below establish his divine credentials? And had not the psalmist also promised: "God will send angels to protect you, lest you dash your foot against a stone?" Insistently the Tempter holds out the jeweled prospect of fame.

Still, does not history show that earthly fame is often bought at the price of personal integrity? And does not scripture insist: "You shall not tempt the Lord your God?" Back Into the teeth of the unseen Tempter Jesus flings the word,

You shall not tempt the Lord your God!

Distant canyons call back

. . . not tempt the Lord your God!

In near exhaustion Jesus climbs the peak of Pisgah, summit from which Moses, himself forbidden to cross into the Promised Land, once viewed the whole Jordan valley. Here Israel's great founder dreamed his valedictory dream of a nation where God alone would be king and the people God's obedient disciples. From this commanding summit Jesus surveys the land stretching westward to the heights of Jerusalem, then beyond to the Great Sea. Shrouded in distant mists lie Athens of fabled grandeur, Rome, epitome of worldly glory and military might, Alexandria, storehouse of vast learning, and northward, past towering Hermon, Antioch, eastern nerve-center of Rome's sprawling imperium.

Israel knows only too well the crush of Rome's iron heel and the blows of her mailed fists. Row upon row of crosses at Judean and Galilean crossroads bear mute testimony to Rome's callous disregard of human life and worth. With God's promise and peoples' discontent as his rallying cry, might not Jesus summon an army of faithful warriors to throw off, once and for all, the bitter yoke of the hated oppressor? Might not he, like Alexander before him, lead legions to the very edges of the eastern world to establish God's Kingdom on earth? Would not Israel then finally be seen as the true Light of the World? And did not the words of the Coronation Psalm, lately heard amid the baptismal downpour, mark him out as conqueror?

> *I have set my king on my holy hill. Ask me and I will give you the heathen for your inheritance, the uttermost parts of earth for your possession!*

Indeed, had not his own dear mother long ago confided in awe, that his name — Yeshua, Joshua, Jesus, Deliverer, Savior — had been whispered to her by an angel of God?

Once again the Tempter's voice is heard:

> *All this power and glory I will give to you, for it is mine to give. Fall down and worship me. Reach out and the world can be yours.*

Yet not the marching drum-beat of armies, but the subdued strain pf Isaiah's Song of the Suffering Servant, sounds through Jesus' consciousness. Had not that mighty prophet of redemption promised that one called Immanuel, "God with us," would also be called "Prince of Peace?" And what will it profit man or nation to gain the whole world and lose one's soul? The word of Micah rings clear:

> *Not by might nor by power but by my Spirit says the Lord of Hosts.*

With that, the vision of the Kingdom comes to focus:

He has borne our griefs and carried our sorrows, and
by his stripes we are healed.

Nothing less than a campaign of humility, healing, and service will bring true liberation and ultimate security to the land. Jesus will be Israel's Servant King. He will seek no glory save the glory of God and the salvation of God's people. He will lead his followers in a campaign of compassion, and in their response God's rule will become visible.

One final time he shakes his fist in the face of the unseen tempter. One final time his voice rises in defiance. One final time the crags and canyons echo the words of a soul now confident of mission:

You shall worship the Lord your God, and him alone
shall you serve . . . him alone shall you serve!

His fasting complete, he rises, strengthened in spirit for whatever tomorrow will bring. Today still offers daylight enough for refreshment at the fruit stalls of Jericho. A resolute, confident Jesus of Nazareth sets his face northward toward Galilee.

This retelling is based on Mark chapter 1, Matthew chapter 4 and Luke chapter 4.

----

21. WE NEVER HEARD IT LIKE THIS!

Possibly no other sermon has influenced so many hearers as the one in this story. Called variously "Sermon on the Mount" and "Sermon on the Plain," its sayings were, no doubt, repeated on many a hill and many a plain, across the length and breadth of Galilee.

The traveler loses no time making his way northward, along the well-traveled east road of the River Jordan. In village after village he is greeted with the news: John the Baptizer has been seized by King Herod and thrown into the royal dungeon.

Herod is "king" in the land but only through the graces of Rome. A toadying vassal, Herod lives at Machaerus, a military castle-fort perched atop a promontory overlooking the Dead Sea, a stronghold constructed by his illustrious grandfather, Herod the Great. For what crime has this petty ruler dared seize charismatic John and imprison him? John has spoken out fearlessly against Herod's adulterous marriage to his sister-in-law; such preaching the king will not allow. The crowds of Judea which until now have listened eagerly for John's every word will no more hear that challenging voice "crying in the wilderness."

The traveler quickens his pace as he approaches Galilee, his own home province. No time must be lost, the Spirit burns within his soul. His own voice must now become the trumpet proclaiming the Jubilee Year of God's favor, liberation through the Heavenly Kingdom.

Begin at Nazareth? Not that. His own hometown offers little support from which to launch a campaign of this magnitude. And without doubt the old saying holds true, "No prophet is honored in his own hometown." Capernaum offers more promising opportunity and must become his headquarters; Capernaum, commercial crossroad at the northern end of Lake Galilee, trading junction on the well traveled *Via Maris*, "Way of the Sea," caravan route to the Mediterranean and beyond. Here each day, dozens of camel trains shuttle between Damascus in Syria and Alexandria in North Africa. From Capernaum word of the Kingdom can go out in all compass directions. Here disciples may be found to study and promote the new Kingdom's goals. Here, above all, he will find crowds waiting to listen, some already baptized by John, multitudes eager to hear of a way out of their misery, poverty, sickness and oppression, eager to hear once more of that covenant made by God with his Chosen People, eager to recall the glory of the country's mighty kings. Capernaum it must be.

Not a moment to be lost. Announcements must be posted and shouted out by town-criers. On a grassy hillside just outside the city a crowd is already forming to hear what this unknown preacher from Nazareth may have to say. A mixed assembly, one would describe them: here and there a handful of well-dressed townspeople, but the great majority obviously poor, many wearing clothes little better than rags, more than a few whose sunken cheeks mark them as hungry for just a decent meal.

They prick up their ears as the man from Nazareth calls for

attention:

> *You poor people there — you are blessed, you know.*
> *Heaven's Kingdom is for you!*
> *You mourners — you are blessed. You will dry those*
> *tears!*
> *You humble folks — you are blessed. You will inherit*
> *the earth!*
> *You hungry and thirsty people are blessed. You will*
> *eat and drink your fill of righteousness!.*
> *You merciful folks — you are blessed. You will have*
> *mercy shown to you!*
> *You people of sincere hearts — you are blessed.*
> *You will be given a vision of God!*
> *You peacemakers — oh, you are blessed. You will be*
> *called children of God!*
> *Consider yourselves fortunate when others persecute*
> *you on account of the Kingdom. Be happy at such*
> *treatment; it puts you in the company of the prophets*
> *who were persecuted in their own day!*

The crowd has grown still, no one milling about any more. They strain to take in every word. Never before have they heard preaching like this. What kind of man is this Nazarene? What sort of kingdom is he proposing?

Do his words make any sense? Doesn't everyone know it is the rich, not the poor, who get the breaks in this world? The powerful who inherit whatever good the earth has to offer? The hardnosed, not the humble, who make their way to the top? Priests and scribes, certainly not common folks, who gain the ear of God? Is this preacher trying to suggest that the chief goal in life is not to gain power, not to accumulate wealth, not to climb the ladder of privilege, not to swear vengeance on one's enemies; instead to strive for humility, consideration and compassion for the needs and feelings of others?

That seems to be exactly what their ears are hearing.
They turn to each other and draw in their breath.

*All of you out there — you are the ones chosen to
build the New Israel. You are the light of the world!
You are the salt of the earth! You are going to help
this nation achieve its God-given high calling. I'm
challenging you — live up to your high calling!*

*Don't get me wrong: Don't think I am saying disre-
gard the Commandments of God, tone them down,
ignore them, forget them — not on your life. I am
saying, keep the Law completely as God intended it
to be kept — down to the crossing of each 't' and
dotting of each 'i'. That is the only way our country
can become truly free!*

*Take another look at The Ten Commandments —
you know them well. 'You shall not kill, commit
no murder.' Now you might say to me, I've never
murdered anybody, I'm clean at least on that score.
Well let me tell you, there are more ways to kill than
by hitting your brother over the head with a rock or
stabbing him in the belly with a dagger. Rage in your
heart, looking for ways to strike back, vowing ven-
geance — these are murder, too. That kind of killing
goes on all the time in high places and low.*

*So, set things right with your estranged brother or
sister before you even consider religious duties. When
you fall out with someone, settle the argument then
and there. Religious duties? Let them wait; reconcili-
ation is paramount and time is of the essence. Before*

you know it, opportunity slips away and you might find yourself in jail. Think about these things when you say, "I've never killed anybody."

People have been saying since way back when: "An eye for an eye, a tooth for a tooth." You may tell me, these exact words can be found in the Torah, so they must be God's way, practice them. If someone hits you, hit him right back; if he gouges out an eye, gouge out one of his; if he knocks out two of your teeth, go after two of his. For God's sake, that is precisely what God is not saying. These words were never intended as license for revenge, for paying back one wrong with another wrong. These words were given to prevent the escalation of violence, to settle grievances before they get completely out of hand, to keep petty disputes from escalating into tribal feuds or full scale warfare. For God's sake, seek a kindlier way.

My message to you is: do not resist evil at all! When someone hits you on your right cheek, turn your left cheek to him as well. When that Roman soldier detains you on the street and forces you — by regulation, I know — to carry his rucksack one mile, smile and offer to carry it a second mile; that's not going to kill you. Let's show those Romans that we Jews have a law such as they, with all their vaunted courts, never thought of having.

As for all those Roman generals and their troops stationed here at our expense, people have been saying for years, "Love your neighbor, hate your enemy." Now please, don't tell me those words are found in the Torah, because they absolutely are not found there. God never even hinted at such a hate-based

111

attitude and never will. What God did say and what I am saying to you is: Love your enemies! Pray for those who treat you miserably and persecute you! That is God's way, and I am saying, that has got to be your way.

Look how God treats everybody alike with kindness— scoundrels as well as decent folks, even those who refuse to recognize that God exists at all. The Father up there showers gifts on everybody alike — good folks, bad folks — rain when needed, sun when required. Now if God draws no line between, as we say, friend and foe, neither should you. When you draw your circle of concern, draw it big enough to include the enemy, too. That's what being perfect is — accepting other people as they are, warts and all. If you stick with me, before we finish you will have a whole new concept of who is enemy and who is friend.

Don't judge other people even in your thought, lest you yourself be judged. The measure you use in forming opinions about others will be the measure other people use to form their opinion of you.

Always begin by taking a good look at your own face in the mirror. You might think you are pretty adept at picking out the dust speck from somebody else's eye, but don't you see that big branch sticking right into your own eye? "Brother," you keep saying, "here, let me get that speck out of your eye!" And all the while you have that huge branch poking straight into your own eye. Ha! First get rid of that branch, then your vision will be good enough to go after specks in other people's eyes. Understanding

*one's own imperfect self – that is key to facing other
people's imperfections. That is the starting point for
those who would truly like to get along with God and
with each other.*

The Man from Nazareth draws a deep breath, then takes
a long drink from a water-skin held aloft by a friendly hand. A
buzz runs through the crowd like that of a bee colony beginning
to swarm. Listeners look at each other dumbfounded, simply
shaking their heads. Never before have they heard preaching
like this. This man is speaking with the air of authority from
God. A few shrug their shoulders and quickly slip away, but
most linger and insist they will be back. They can hardly wait
to hear more.

Their friends have got to hear this man, too.

This retelling is based on Matthew chapters 5-7 and Luke chapter 6.

----

22. PARTYING WITH SINNERS

A tax official at Capernaum decides he can take no more of Jesus' sermons. A surprise visit persuades him to change his mind.

Levi Matthew, newly appointed supervisor of the Caravan Revenue Section, Capernaum, cannot shake Jesus of Nazareth from his mind. That preacher upsets Levi Matthew no end. He thinks about him as he sits down to dinner with friends in his spacious home overlooking Lake Galilee. He thinks about him as he sits in the tax kiosk at the main crossing on the *Via Maris*.

Levi Matthew, we should note, is a young Jew of considerable talent and ambition, yet is not at all well regarded in his home town, Capernaum. Put more bluntly, to many of his neighbors Levi Matthew is 'scum'. Rome, you see, controls Israel, as well as every other nation in the Mediterranean Basin. Tax rates for each district are levied directly by the Senate in Rome, but the nitty-gritty of collecting revenue in each locale is left to local operators. These operators in turn 'farm out' the actual collecting to entrepreneurs willing to bear the stigma that goes along with such despised work. These entrepreneurs are allowed considerable leeway — discretionary powers — room for gouging or for cutting deals on the side. So, if the people at large hate Rome for a hundred different reasons — and that they do — then they hate even more those of their own neighbors who stoop to exact their hard earned shekels to send away, so Rome can send in more troops. On the 'Desirable Career' scale, tax-collector scores as close to zero as you can get. And that is exactly the career path that Levi Matthew has chosen for himself.

"How," you might ask this young man to his face, "how can you, supposedly a devout, believing Jew, square what you are doing with your faith and conscience?" He will give you a straight answer, "Not easily. But bear in mind, one need not stick with one job forever. I already own that large house on the hill overlooking the eastern shore, servants to staff the place, riding horses in my stable, and a pleasure boat in the marina below. True, people call me names behind my back and sometimes directly to my face. But in a very few years my fortune will be made, and I will move elsewhere. New friends don't inquire how you made your money; they just want to help you spend it. With money comes power and with power comes prestige. I know what I want and I know how to go after it. One day, I will be recognized in Jerusalem as a great man, a benefactor in Israel."

All of which makes that new preacher, Jesus of Nazareth, with his talk of poverty and meekness, so irksome to Levi Matthew. And that is why, after hearing Jesus once and then a second time, Levi Matthew has simply decided, never again.

Until this particular morning when, sitting at his kiosk desk, Levi sees a shadow at the door. At first he does not bother even to look up, it will be just another caravan driver arriving early to haggle over his toll. When Levi finally does look up, he is thunderstruck to see that preacher, Jesus, standing in his doorway. For a time the Nazarene says not a word. When at length he does speak, his words strike the tax-man like a lightning bolt: "Levi Matthew, you are the kind of disciple I am looking for. Follow me in the campaign for the Kingdom of Heaven!"

For as long as he may live, Levi Matthew will never be able to fully describe the feeling that sweeps over him in that moment. "What could this preacher, who insists on God's law being fulfilled to the final letter, possibly want with a person of my reputation? Is he making some funny joke at my expense? Or could he be so naive as to actually think that a tax farmer might be an asset to his campaign?"

For a long moment the gaze between the two does not falter. Then, in a manner Levi will never be able to put into adequate words, his inward doubt dissolves; this preacher is actually offering him a position. And to his own amazement Levi finds himself thinking, "I want to do this. I am going to follow this man. My long-term career plan can be put on hold until I have a chance to explore and evaluate this New Kingdom." Then, without so much as looking down, Levi Matthew snaps shut his ledger, pushes it aside, rises and follows Jesus of Nazareth out the door.

Levi understands vaguely what is involved. To begin with, his house and other holdings must be put up for sale. Proceeds of the sale will go not to Jesus but to the poor of the community. For his own part, Levi senses, he has something critical he can contribute to the movement: his influence with the Capernaum religious leaders, the Pharisees. These Pharisees owe him something from past dealings. They have influence and connections to advance the cause. With the Pharisees solidly behind the Kingdom, there is no telling how far Jesus can go. Levi determines to invite local Pharisees to his farewell feast and introduce them informally to Jesus. Invitations are sent out promptly to friends from the tax community, as well as to local business acquaintances. This feast, Matthew is determined, will be an event not to be forgotten. Nothing must be spared.

On the appointed afternoon, guests begin arriving early, too many at any single moment for host Levi Matthew to greet personally But from the outset Levi Matthew senses that his guests are not mixing well. For one thing, the Pharisees seem to have misgivings about the company they have gotten into. They are especially irked to see that young Nazarene preacher associating freely among the tax people. When other of Jesus' recruits arrive, these Pharisees put their grievance directly to the recruits: should this man they are joining up with be seen associating with bottom-rung society, to the extent of eating with them? Is this the way to show regard for God's righteous Law and set an example as Light for the World?

When Jesus' recruits look helplessly at each other, unprepared for such confrontation, Jesus comes to their rescue, extending his hand to the Pharisees and introducing himself. "I'm here," he explains, "not for healthy folks, you see, but for the sick ones. I'm making a house call, you might say, on Levi Matthew and his tax-office friends. Do you remember how our prophet Hosea put it: 'I desire not sacrifice but a show of love, understanding rather than burnt offerings?'"

The Pharisees sputter in their cocktails. To be addressed in such fashion is not what they are accustomed to. By now, Levi Matthew realizes, things are not going well. He claps his hands to interrupt, "Let's all go inside and see what the chef has fixed for us. You'll be delighted!" The sumptuous buffet of roasts, fruits, salads, desserts, and wines will surely set things onto a smoother track.

But hardly have various groups settled down than some of John the Baptizer's supporters begin questioning Jesus about his views on fasting: "John said avoid rich foods. In fact, his schedule appoints this very day as a fast day. Jesus, you and your followers don't seem to follow a fasting regimen, why not?"

At that moment, a waitress comes by offering goblets with wine. She lifts her bulging wineskin high and directs the spigot into each empty goblet. Jesus seizes the metaphor: "No wine maker would ever attempt to store new wine in old wineskins, unless he wanted to risk a royal mess! New wine demands new skins, strong enough to handle fermentation."

Then, observing people wearing their party finery, he continues, "Tailors don't sew new cloth onto worn out clothing; that would only be inviting larger rips."

Finally, to doubly underscore it all:

> At a wedding feast, the father of the bride does not pinch shekels. He treats guests to the finest of fare. Then when the bridal couple have finally slipped away and the guests gone home, the father sits down to tally up the bills, shakes his head, and groans, we've got to stop eating!

Laughter greets this last. But the Pharisees, who have been squirming all along, are not in the least amused. Obviously Jesus is throwing bad light on their time-honored observances. From now on, this subject of ritual will be a bone of contention between them and this Nazarene. Does not God specifically command his people to observe established traditions? Can traditions somehow be jettisoned each time something new comes along? Have they not heard Jesus himself insisting the Torah must be fulfilled to the dotting of each 'i' and crossing of each 't'? So, how can you observe the Torah properly if you relax rules in the name of changing times?

The issue will surface again and again as the Kingdom campaign moves forward. God's ordinances came carved on the stones of Sinai, but what if the times and place no longer fit the carving? What happens when irresistible change meets immovable tradition? Garments will be ripped, wine spilled — yes, and blood — before this issue is resolved.

And parties will break up early.

Levi Matthew's "feast to end all feasts" is rapidly falling apart. The Pharisees have gathered up their robes and left in a huff. Other guests, embarrassed by it all, have been shaking Levi Matthew's hand, saying they must be off to look after pressing matters. "Good luck in your new venture," they murmur, as they hurry to the door.

Obviously, things have not gone as planned. Yet, truth be told, Levi Matthew is not unhappy. He is convinced he has made the right choice in deciding to follow Jesus. His blood runs warm and not just from wine. No question, but Jesus understands his position — tax-people are not to be considered 'scum'. Did he not hear Jesus say in so many words,

> *I have not come to call righteous people but sinners to repentance?*

Deep in his soul Levi Matthew is a happy man.

This retelling is based on Mark chapter 2, Matthew chapter 9 and Luke chapter 5.

THE INN:
Deep in the Den

That morning I could not sleep past the first glimmer of light. Abby only grunted as she heard me climb into my clothes. I whispered, "I'll be down in the reading room checking out some books." More honestly, I just needed to get away by myself to think through things Lisa had suggested during her story-time the evening before. Lisa had surprised me.

Lisa, you recall, is doing field research toward her degree in psychology at the University of Montana. As I say, the young lady surprised me with her line of questions.

The Reading Room was just off the great room and fireplace. They might better have called it Reading Nook, since it was only big enough for one small table and two simple chairs; walls were completely covered with shelves loaded with books. I took down one or two at random, and laid them on the table in front of me.

Lisa had described a course she had taken, centered on Elisabeth Kubler-Ross and her widely publicized Stages of Grief: denial, anger, bargaining, depression, and acceptance. Kubler-Ross had made the point that while these five stages were generally descriptive of the grieving process connected with death, they did not necessarily all apply to every bereavement situation or occur in the same succession. Also they might well describe working through personal loss other than that associated with death.

On that last point, Lisa zeroed in: Might these five stages of grief apply somehow to rifts occurring among family or friends? Might people, once on intimate terms but lately turned antagonistic toward each other, somehow be experiencing the grieving process? Might they be going through denial, anger, bargaining, depression, and acceptance? Thus Lisa, working toward her university requirements, was asking me to consider the absurd possibility that I might somehow be grieving over my split with Allison and Ron!

Denial? Admittedly, I had denied reality when I first heard of their spending nights together. That simply could not have been true, but then, it was true.

Anger? Yes, I admit I was piss-angry at the time, and still am after all this time. Wouldn't you be?

Bargaining? I never could figure exactly what Kubler Ross had in mind with attempting to bargain grief away; I'll have to pass on that one.

Depression? How could I deny my state of mind? Seven long years of hurting, yes. Not that I wanted my funk to show in front of people, but they could see it. I know they could see it, the whole seven years' worth.

Acceptance? I suppose, that too, I had finally accepted that we would never be speaking decently to each other again. That Saturday afternoon, when I met Abby and asked if we might start seeing each other, I was finally admitting to myself and everybody else that Allison and Ron were out of my life forever..

So Lisa had convinced me, in spite of myself, I had been going through the five stages of grieving.

But at that very moment she had come back with her blindsiding question. She asked — not me individually, of course, but the whole group for the sake of her study — did we really <u>*want to*</u> *reach the point of ac-*

ceptance, where we would be satisfied that family or friends were split off forever and there could never be a re-connecting? Is that the kind of mental and emotional adjustment we were hoping for?

To that question my answer had to be no and yes. No, of course I don't want to be cut off from those two girls of mine. I miss them terribly when I come home to an empty house at night, and I will never resign myself to that once-a-month visiting arrangement I managed to salvage.

But as for Allison and Ron, those two stinking liars, yes, they are gone, simply cut out of my life forever, and good riddance. I would forget them if I could, but damn it, I can't. How could it ever be any different? Grieve for those two? Could you be suggesting, my dear Lisa, that when I wish them to hell, my curses are somehow tears that I am holding back? That one I will need to give lots of thought to. Lots. Someday I will read a review of your dissertation in a magazine and maybe understand your way of thinking better then than I possibly can now.

I slipped my books back onto the shelf and moved over to the great room, just to sit and stare into the cold fireplace. Ashes from last night's fire still lay heaped on the great hearth, waiting for Kori to come shovel them away. Here and there a lick of flame would appear for an instant, then disappear – a tiny flicker along with a pop, just a pop, but loud against the great room's otherwise silence. A bit of unburned firewood insisting, "Well, what do you know, I was still alive in all these ashes!"

So now, the stupid ashes are trying to talk to me! Why do I even listen to all this stuff and just get more and more mixed up?

I glanced at my watch. Abby must be almost dressed for breakfast. I headed for the stairs.

----

23. A QUADRIPLEGIC WALKS AGAIN

Host Levi Matthew begins his set of stories. He says, that with our permission, he will turn the floor over to his namesake from the gospels to describe events as he might have witnessed them firsthand. So, to begin, a word about the disciple Levi Matthew:

Actually, there is little more to be said. Half a dozen sentences in the gospels constitute his entire biography, and these we have already shared. We do find the man's name (or names) included in the various listings of Jesus' Twelve, and that is the extent of it; beyond these rosters never another specific mention about the man or any word from his lips. In the drama of the gospels Levi Matthew's role remains a modest one.

As for our combining his two names into one (as the gospels never actually do), in certain of the listings the man is referred to as Levi, in others as Matthew, not at all an uncommon occurrence. Apparently the two describe the same person. Just so you are aware, we choose to link the two names together and listen as Levi Matthew now begins his story:

I first met Tom at my farewell party in Capernaum, where he was among the recruits for Jesus' School. From our very first handshake, the two of us hit it off. He was a practical sort, more so than I. He could size up a situation and say, this needs to be done now, or that, so let's get at it. When he learned, for example, that I was putting my house up for sale, Tom said, "I know an agent in town who can handle that." Then he hunted up the agent, and even read through the obscure parts of the sales contract.

One morning, Tom burst in, "We must get over to Jesus' place: it's been jammed since daybreak." We knew very well the crowds that gathered evenings on the hillsides outside town. Now more and more, crowds were also gathering by day at Jesus' house in town, people hoping to find healing.

It had started the very day Jesus took up residence in Capernaum. At the synagogue he had gathered a small group for a study session. Barely had they said good morning, when this disoriented man burst in and began yelling, "What in God's name are you doing here, you Nazarene? Have you come over here to destroy us?"

Jesus walked over to the man and demanded,

Shut your mouth, come out of him!

Now you might wonder, exactly who was Jesus talking to when he shouted, "Come out of him?" It was whatever had taken control of that man — 'an unclean spirit' was the way we described it. Very likely you would offer some different, contemporary diagnosis, well and good. At any rate, this spirit, this power, had invaded the man's mind and taken control of him.

Hearing Jesus' shout, the man went into convulsion, writhing and flailing, right there on the synagogue floor. Moments later he snapped out of it and opened his eyes, quite amazed to realize that his ailment was gone. The others in that synagogue were dumbfounded. They sensed immense charisma, authority, behind Jesus' command. With no more than a barked order he had restored that troubled man to sound health.

The news of that incident went blazing through town. Within hours, scores of sick folk were crowding around Jesus' door, requesting to be healed. "He has power from God," they were saying. "I want him to cure my fever," or "I hope he can help my little boy." All kinds of requests.

Which at once created a dilemma for Jesus. A day has only so many hours, while the number of sick people hoping to be healed on any given day can expand *ad infinitum*. The Capernaum crowds kept growing at an alarming rate. We did have doctors in town, but their fees were beyond the means of most people. When illness would strike, families would soon exhaust their resources, then watch the illness run its course and take its toll. But, here was a preacher drawing on God's power, asking no fee, but, out of the goodness of his heart, taking people's problems to be his own.

Yet healing was not Jesus' declared mission. He was called, he insisted, to proclaim the Kingdom of Heaven. Consequently, whenever healings did occur, he would do his best to play them down. "Keep quiet about this," he would say to the person he had helped. "Go to the town officials, ask for your clean bill of health but don't breathe another word to anyone else." Which was like telling the wind to stop blowing. People simply do not keep quiet when they have been cured. News of Jesus' power was soon spreading beyond Capernaum, drawing more and more sick folks in from neighboring towns.

As Tom and I approached Jesus' place that morning, people were standing six deep outside the door. Four young men had just arrived with a litter on which they carried a friend, paralyzed from the neck down. Blocked by the crowd from getting near the door, these four had hoisted their friend up onto the roof. Now they were loosening roof tiles and lowering the man on ropes into that packed house.

For the moment Jesus said, "Back off, back off, give this man some air." Then turning to the paralyzed youth he said,

Friend, your sins are forgiven you.

Mixed into that crowd were a number of Pharisees, there to make sure things stayed on track. These Pharisees were more than a little miffed when they heard Jesus say, "Your sins are forgiven you."

Just who does this Nazarene think he is — God? The man is blaspheming!

Sensing their reaction, Jesus turned to the Pharisees and asked, "Well, which is easier to say: 'Your sins are forgiven,' or, 'Get up and walk?' But that you may know that the Son of Man does have authority on earth to forgive sins," — now he turned back to the paraplegic — "Friend, stand up, roll up that litter of yours and head for home." Which is exactly what the young man was now able to do.

The crowd gasped in sheer amazement:

Incredible! We have never seen the like -- God sharing divine power with people!

For weeks afterward, Tom and I talked about the incident, struck by the manner in which Jesus had linked healing and forgiving, as if they were one and the same: "Your sins are forgiven! Get up and walk." Was he implying that the young man's paralysis had been induced by some sin, so that once that sin was removed, the paralysis might disappear? Take away sin and you take away sickness?

Each of us could name acquaintances who, through debauchery, had wasted their health and succumbed to illness. On the other hand, we also knew decent folks who had led exemplary lives, yet had been struck down by crippling disease. Had these also somehow brought illness on themselves? We simply could not conclude that sickness is the inevitable result of sin.

We chanced, one morning, to pass a blind man begging by the roadside. This man, so we were told, had been blind since birth. So, who, we wondered, could possibly have committed the sin that brought on the man's blindness? Was he somehow being made to suffer for his parents' sins? From whatever angle we looked, illness was neither explainable nor fair.

When we put the question to Jesus, he replied,

> *You'll never pin that answer down. Neither this man*
> *nor his parents sinned that he should be born blind.*
> *It happened in order that the works of God might be*
> *clearly seen.*

Then and there he gave that man sight for the first time in his life. So, our questions remained basically without answers. Yet again and again we would witness such wonders of healing occurring before our eyes, and hear promise of more wonders to come. Repeatedly Jesus would challenge us,

The works you see me doing, you will be doing too;
in fact, greater works than these.

At times, especially later on, we did find ourselves able to heal, yet those occasions were rare. And we were learning.

It takes deep faith and patience to face illness. It takes deep faith and patience to care for those who must endure illness. And it takes deep faith to reach for the power of God to seize each day's discoveries and opportunities and do something significant with them. Human beings are given increasing power to combine knowledge, research, resources, and skills to confront the forces that undermine health. Faith and compassion combine to challenge illnesses before which otherwise we would stand helpless. Then we marvel and praise God who works wonders among his people.

Yes, forgiveness is healing. And healing isforgiveness.
When we ask for one, we ask for the other.
And God is always ready to hear our prayer.

This retelling is based on Mark chapter 2, Matthew chapter 9 and John chapter 5.

----

24. PRAYER TO UNITE THE WORLD

Levi Matthew learns a prayer which he will share with many. These many will share with more, until that prayer spins a world-wide web of faith and concern.

We were ready to leave Capernaum early that morning, but strangely Jesus was nowhere to be seen. He had instructed us in so many words: "Be at my quarters at sunrise, ready to head on out." The twelve of us had arrived at the crack of dawn, but now Jesus himself was nowhere to be seen, nor had anyone seen him since the evening before. We waited impatiently, spending the time learning to know one another.

We were the dozen called by Jesus out of his crowd of listeners to form his School of Twelve. Each had a word to share about his previous work and how he had on the spur of the moment decided to take leave of career and family.

Two brothers, Simon and Andrew, had operated a fishing business; when Jesus said he wanted them to 'fish for people,' they had promptly put their boat up for sale and joined the venture. James and John, also brothers, had likewise been part of a fishing business along with their father, Zebedee; responding to Jesus' call, they had at once thrown their nets across their boat and started after him. Philip had been a rabbinical student. Hailing from Bethsaida, the same tiny fishing village as the four already mentioned, he had recently moved into a dormitory at the Capernaum Rabbinical Institute, and now had decided to go with Jesus. Nathanael Bartholemew, close friend of Philip, had likewise been a student. Thomas (that's Tom, you've already met him) had been partner with his twin brother in a fruit export firm. James Alphaeus (notice we had two Jameses), like Jesus, had been a carpenter. Simon the Zealot (don't confuse him with Simon Peter) had organized political rallies in Galilee. Two others also shared a common name, Judas: Judas Thaddaeus who had worked at various trades in Capernaum. All eleven mentioned thus far (including myself) were from our northern province, Galilee. The lone exception was our other Judas who hailed from Kerioth in Judea. He had served a brief career in finance. You can see what a motley lot we were – each deeply excited about following Jesus and the Kingdom cause, yet each apprehensive as to how we could get along with each other on a day-to-day basis.

As we talked, a small crowd of townspeople had been arriving with sick friends, hoping Jesus might heal them. These jostled for position at the door.

Simon Peter had just announced he would go looking, when Jesus came in from the road, hair and clothes dripping from the shower he'd been running through. He had spent the whole night in prayer in the hills outside the city, had gone there seeking solitude and then stayed the night through, pouring out his soul to Heaven for guidance. Now the man was throbbing with energy, anxious to get out onto the road.

First, he asked us twelve recruits to kneel in a circle around him, while friends gathered close by. Then he spoke words from a Psalm:

> *Behold, how good and pleasant it is for siblings to dwell together in unity!*

He went on to quote another psalm, which some of us recalled having sung at John's baptismal camp:

> *This is the day which the Lord has made; let us rejoice and be glad in it. Save us, we beseech thee, O Lord! O Lord, grant success!*

That psalm was to become our theme song, sung again and again at many a stop along the campaign trail.

Around the circle Jesus went, embracing each one, calling each by name and looking searchingly into our eyes. Then he prayed for God's Spirit on us all – not forgetting those friends who would be staying in Capernaum and friends still to be met who would soon hear about the New Kingdom. He commended all alike to the care of Heaven.

Then we broke away, heading eastward along the *Via Maris*, and south through the villages that border the eastern shore of the lake.

That first night out was spent in a farmer's barn, something which I confess, was entirely new for me. Even before we bunked down on the hay, I began to miss my bed and linen sheets. "Was I up to this?" I wondered. I compared notes with Tom who had similar misgivings. Inwardly I breathed a prayer of my own: "God, I hope I have made the right decision; make me equal to whatever this is going to take." To this day whenever I smell new-mown hay, it brings back that first uneasy night on the road. I was determined to adjust.

Next morning things looked brighter. There was breakfast served by our host and his wife – corn grits and fish, netted in the lake just before daylight.

After the meal, Jesus sketched our training program, how we would be spending major portions of each day. During morning hours, there would be group study with open discussion. Afternoons would be spent visiting village squares, meeting people and setting up rallies to be held at sundown. Following the evening rallies, we would gather for late prayers, and then bed down in whatever quarters would be provided.

I have to smile when I tell you all this, because it was a rare day, indeed, when this plan worked out the way it was supposed to. Almost without exception there were interruptions, as word went out that Jesus was on the way. People would beg off from work to intercept him with pleas about their sicknesses and other woes. He had a heart for these people, "Our study session," he would apologize, "can be put on hold until tomorrow, but these people with their hurts are here and now; we may never see them again, so we've got to do what we can, when and as we can." Yet when townspeople would beg him to stay on in their villages for longer than a day or two, he would say no, insisting we were on a tight schedule and must move on to other towns already waiting for us. Thus the next two years were to become a constant whirl of saying hello and saying goodbye in the midst of a hundred *ad hoc* adjustments.

At prayer time next morning, one of our group asked Jesus, "Would you teach us to pray, the way John taught his followers?" Some remembered those routines and recitations from the Jordan camp meetings. Jesus seemed ready for the request:

*I do have a prayer for you, a simple prayer to God
that the New Kingdom will arrive and that you will
be ready to help make it happen. You can teach these
few words to new recruits and you can use them to
frame your own private prayers.*

Then, for the first time ever, we heard those fifty words destined
to circle the world. I, for one, would teach these words to hundreds at crossroad gatherings; those who heard them would
repeat them to hundreds more, until those few words, released
to the wind, would take root in all sorts of soil – homes, businesses, friendship circles, tribal councils, international consultations. At this moment we may suppose, they are being lifted
in a thousand different places in a thousand different tongues,
as cords which bind human souls to each other and to God are
drawn tight. Here are the words he taught us:

*Our Father in heaven, hallowed be your name.
Your Kingdom come, Your will be done on earth as in heaven.
Give us today our daily bread.
Forgive us our sins as we forgive those who sin against us.
Save us from the time of trial and deliver us from evil.* *

In the hectic rush and crush of the two years to follow, we
would need that prayer, fervently spoken, to enable us to work
as a team. Tucked into the heart of those few lines was that
petition enabling us to live and work together:

Forgive us our sins as we forgive those who sin against us.

That petition would mould our mixed crew into a working
team. We would plead for forgiveness from God and then
share forgiveness with each other and many beyond.

I have no doubt that in your time too, people the world around are drawn to God and each other through this prayer. Couples pray it at wedding altars and in their homes, business partners in their offices and factories, diplomats as they face issues of state, travelers as they sail or fly, warriors faced with hardship and death. Translated into every tongue, and given substance in the lives of those who speak them, these words bind human hearts to God and to each other:

Forgive us our sins, as we forgive those who sin against us.

This retelling is based on Matthew chapter 6 and Luke chapter 11.
*English Language Liturgical Consultation, 1988

----

25. WHEN ENEMIES ARE NEIGHBORS

*Much of Jesus' teaching came in the form of parables —
homely word-pictures describing workaday situations, but
intended to convey deep, spiritual truths. Listeners would
find such earthy illustrations easy to remember and pass
along; opponents, however, would latch onto little incrimi-
nating evidence. How do you prove heresy from the picture
of a housewife baking bread or a farmer scattering seed on
his field?*

You may have, at some time or other, spoken of a helpful per-
son as a Good Samaritan. That strikes me as very odd, since
in my time, we would never have set those two words Good
and Samaritan side by side. Samaritans were not good, they
were bad. Call someone a Samaritan and you were running
him into the dirt. Jesus had the 'S' word thrown at him repeat-
edly by opponents – "You no-good Samaritan!" To be aware of
this widespread prejudice of ours may help you understand the
impact of this story as Jesus told it.

It was late one evening in the village where we'd been work-
ing, the rally just about ready to break up. A man from town

shouted, "Question, question!" This man was a lawyer, well trained in matters of the Torah, highly respected in that village. Jesus asked the crowd to quiet down, long enough to hear the man's question. It was: "What must I do to gain eternal life?"

That question seemed fair enough, especially when Jesus tossed it right back into the man's own court of expertise: "What does the Torah have to say? What do you read there?" The man summed up the two tables of the Law as neatly as any rabbi in our synagogues might have done:

> Love the Lord your God with all your heart, all your soul and all your mind; then love your neighbor as yourself.

Jesus' reply was enthusiastic:

> Right on, Man! Do that and you have it made – life will be yours!

You may already have guessed, since that man was a lawyer, he was prepared with a follow-up question, "And who, Sir, exactly is my neighbor?" Semantics, semantics! "Would my neighbor be the person living next door? My close kinsman? My fellow villager? My fellow tribesperson? Define 'neighbor' precisely, Jesus, if you can."

The crowd, sensing a spirited debate, went quiet as Jesus began this story. You have heard it many times, I know, but a preliminary word about our local topography and characters involved will help underscore the startling impact that story made on the lawyer and those townspeople – to say nothing of myself and Tom.

The setting was the steep road leading from Jerusalem to Jericho, that twisting, treacherous, 20-mile stretch descending sharply from the Jerusalem Ridge, at elevation 6200 feet *above* sea level, into the Great Rift Valley, 100 feet *below* sea level. The surrounding mountains are principally desert country, notoriously infested with brigands. Solitary travel was strictly not recommended, even for Roman regulars, who had standing orders not to venture there unaccompanied. Nevertheless, the victim in the story does appear to have been traveling alone.

The priest in the story would be a religious official from the line of Moses and Aaron. He might be on his way home after completing some tour of priestly duty at the temple in Jerusalem. The Levite, another religious functionary, might likewise be traveling in some official capacity.

As for the Samaritan, we need to consider that man's racial background to understand why he was so deeply *persona non grata* with us Jews. Centuries earlier, when our Israelite ancestors came back from Babylon, they discovered people from other blood-lines occupying their Jewish homesteads. These foreign settlers had intermarried with those few Jews who escaped deportation, producing a racially mixed breed, Samaritans. To us pure Jews, these mixed-blood cousins were a lesser breed, culturally and religiously inferior. They never did worship with us in Jerusalem where David and Solomon had situated the temple; they maintained their own worship site in the hills to the north.

So much for background, now the story as we heard it that evening:

> *A man was going down from Jerusalem to Jericho,*
> *and fell into the hands of robbers, who stripped him,*
> *beat him, and made off, leaving him half-dead. By*
> *chance a priest was traveling that road. When he saw*

*the wounded man, he passed him by on the other side.
So likewise a Levite, when he came to the place and
saw the man, passed him by on the other side.*

*But a Samaritan, while traveling, came near. When he
saw the poor man, he was moved with pity, went to him
and bandaged his wounds, cleansing them first with oil
and wine. Then lifting the man onto his own beast, he
brought him to an inn and cared for him there. Next
day he gave two coins to the innkeeper, saying, "Keep
right on caring for him. On my way back, I will repay
you whatever more you spend."*

That was the story, to which Jesus quickly added a question:

*Which of those three, do you think, proved neighbor
to the man who fell into the robbers' hands?*

When our lawyer friend heard that question, he did not actu-
ally say the 'S' word aloud, but he did concede, "The one who
showed him mercy."

Jesus nodded and for a moment said nothing more.
Finally he rounded out the story and the rally:

Go, live that way!

In our bunks that night, Tom and I talked late. That a Samari-
tan should be capable of feeling pity for a Jew, risk his own life,
and spend time and money to help one of our kind, had never
entered our minds. Jews were God's Chosen People, while Sa-
maritans, with their questionable ancestry and worship, obvi-
ously were not. Jesus seemed to be implying that blood-lines and

customs are not all that important when it comes to reaching out to a fellow human being in need. Caring for one's neighbor who needs care supersedes racial and religious considerations.

But how far might that word 'neighbor' actually extend? Were Gentile peoples to be thought of as neighbors, too? We looked at each other, not daring to venture an answer to our own question.

I had always considered myself a broadminded individual. When dealing with foreign caravan drivers passing through our Capernaum tax station, I had treated them decently enough. But I would never have dreamed of inviting a Gentile to sleep under my roof or share a dinner at my table. Jesus was asking us to think outside our own racial and religious box.

Still, there has got to be some ultimate limit, some line beyond which the term neighbor no longer applies. Otherwise, how could we claim to be God's 'Chosen People?'

One day our friend Paul of Tarsus would look at a racially mixed fellowship of Jewish and Gentile believers, and declare, "In our fellowship there cannot be Greek and Jew, circumcised and uncircumcised, barbarian, Sythian, slave or free, but Christ is all and in all."

It would take many a parable and many a nudge of the Holy Spirit to move us from where we were to where ultimately we would find ourselves.

This retelling is based on Luke chapter 10.

----

26. A LADY WHO LOVED MUCH

Jesus' teachings often stirred deep emotions — feelings of guilt, embarrassment, gratitude, affection — many more. Levi Matthew describes some of the emotions which stirred the heart of one woman who crept uninvited into the home of a prominent Pharisee.

I never did learn the lady's name, but let me tell you in confidence, she loved Jesus, and displayed her love for him quite openly and awkwardly, some might say, brazenly. We saw her for just a few moments at one of those lavish feasts to which Jesus and our School of Twelve would occasionally be invited. This all took place at the home of one Simon, a prominent Pharisee.

I still harbored the notion that if only we could persuade enough Pharisees to support our cause, the Kingdom movement would spread like wildfire through the land. Pharisees wielded clout in worlds both sacred and secular; they were role models, observed and listened to by many. When this particular dinner invitation came, I was delighted, since, to me at least, it offered one more chance at gathering support among the established leaders of the land.

Simon's home turned out to be a grand place. Food was to be served from a central atrium, while guests reclined at low tables in various anterooms. We found our places in a small alcove near the entrance, where anyone wishing might easily engage Jesus in conversation. Talk buzzed, as talk at parties will, loud at first and then louder.

Hardly anybody noticed this lady slip in, but after a time she became obvious to me, as she knelt near Jesus' feet. She was quietly sobbing, so much so that her tears were falling onto Jesus' feet — tears which she quickly brushed away with her hair which hung uncombed about her shoulders. Presently she drew from her bosom a vial of perfume and began pouring that fragrance over Jesus' feet. The rush of the aroma caught the attention of guests, so much so that conversation hushed momentarily, as heads turned our way. Simon our host, who had kept his eye on this whole procedure, leaned toward friends at his table, muttering, "If this Nazarene were any kind of true prophet, he would realize what sinful trash is over there pawing over him." Simon was just about to move in our direction, when Jesus seized the initiative. "Simon!" he called out loudly, "I have a riddle to share, may I tell it?"

Simon was caught with little choice, "Why yes, Teacher, go ahead." He settled back and the place went quiet as Jesus cleared his throat:

> *A certain moneylender had two debtors: one owed him $500, the other just $5. This moneylender, realizing that neither debtor was in position to pay anything, decided to cancel both debts – wipe them off his books.*

*Now which of those two forgiven debtors, do you
suppose, would feel more gratitude toward that
moneylender?*

For a moment Simon looked quizzically at his friends, not
quite sure where all this might be leading. Then he shrugged
and played uneasily along: "I suppose, the one who had the
bigger debt cancelled?"

Jesus nodded, paused a long, intentional pause, then went on.

Did you happen to notice this lady here beside me?

Well, now that you mention it, I do see her. Why?

*When I arrived here at your home, you sent no water
and towel to freshen my feet; this lady has been wash-
ing my feet with tears and drying them with her own
hair. You did not come over to buss me welcome; she
has hardly stopped kissing my feet. You offered me no
face lotion or hair dressing; she has been pouring her
precious perfume over my feet. All of which says to
me, her sins, which are many, have been forgiven, and
that is the reason she shows such great love. A person
forgiven little would be showing little love.*

Simon was nonplused by this candid thrust. Blushing, he
turned back to his friends with feigned laughter and a dismis-
sive shrug of his shoulders. Conversation resumed, and the
incident seemed closed. But Jesus now turned to the woman
who, trembling and woefully embarrassed, was trying to fade
into the shadows.

*Friend, your sins have been taken away, your faith
has saved you. Now let God straighten out your life*

and give you peace.

Not a single word left that woman's lips the entire time. She simply slipped out the door as quietly as she had slipped in.

We did not linger at Simon's place. We were anxious to get back out among the campers and breathe fresh air. There we knew we would find a welcome, people crowding for just a glimpse of Jesus. They would insist that he say something, even if only a few words. Among the common people he would inevitably receive that kind of welcome, the welcome I had hoped the influential might have chosen to show him.

As for that woman's unspoken confession, I have given a great deal of thought to that. She must have sought out Jesus from deep sorrow over wrongs in her past life. Here she was pouring out her heart in sobs and tears. She must have also felt God's mercy keenly, that she would break open her vial of fragrance that way and pour it recklessly. It was her awkward way of saying thank you to God. As she fled Simon's house, I could see her tiny fists clenched and her head held high.

Many a time I have wondered, if perchance later on, that lady might encounter some other soul burdened by guilt, could she then react toward that person as Jesus had reacted toward her? Could she sense the rejection and contempt of those who consider themselves morally and socially superior? Could she read in that other person's body-language some awkward attempt at confession? If so, perhaps then she would hark back to that afternoon when she herself had slipped impulsively into a lofty Pharisee's house, heard Jesus of Nazareth assure her that her sins were cancelled, and received encouragement toward a better life. Perhaps then she would lift a finger to hush that person's embarrassment, and whisper,

Peace, friend. The Lord will show you the way.

And let that person slip quietly into the shadows.

----

*This retelling is based on Mark chapter 14, Matthew chapter 26
and Luke chapter 7.*

----

27. TWO PRAY, ONE IS HEARD

Did you ever consider how passionately Jesus hated? Hated hypocrisy, that is, hated pretence, hated pride that puts others down in order to build one's self up?

Did you ever consider how passionately Jesus loved? Loved forthrightness, loved seeing people accept themselves for what they are, accept the mercy of God, and in turn accept other people for what they are and share with them God's mercy?

This particular parable from Jesus gave me courage to look into my own heart. As a former tax person myself, I could appreciate how the tax man in the story felt as he stood beating his breast in the shadow of the temple's columns:

> *Two men went into the temple to pray, one a Pharisee, the other a tax collector.*
>
> *The Pharisee stood by himself and prayed, "God, I thank you that I am not like other people —greedy, dishonest, or unfaithful in marriage. I am especially glad not to be like that tax collector over there. I ob-*

serve fast days twice a week, and I give you the tenth of whatever I earn." The tax collector stood off to the side, not deeming himself worthy to so much as glance up toward heaven. He simply beat his breast, and murmured, "God, be merciful to me, a sinner!"

When those two went home, it was the tax collector – not the other – who found the favor of God.

Consider yourself superior to others, and eventually you will be humbled. Humble yourself in God's sight, and eventually you will be lifted up.

Jesus certainly was not deprecating righteous living: God-fearing people ought to conduct themselves honestly, practice charity, and remain true to their marriage vows. But to put on self-righteous airs, flaunt one's piety in public, cover over one's own sin by pointing to the sins of others — such conceit Jesus utterly despised.

At our early Capernaum rallies, Jesus had made much of that very point. "Why do you keep saying, 'Brother, let me remove that dust-speck from your eye, when you can't see the big branch sticking in your own eye?" That line had always produced a good laugh from the crowd because of its absurd exaggeration, but it had always struck home. To compare yourself to other people is to tread a dangerous path; it will undoubtedly convince you what a fine person you are. And make you forget that

God resists the proud, but gives grace to the humble.

Humility is the gateway to the life of forgiveness. Humility allows us to speak honestly to God and speak courageously to those we love and respect. Humility allows us to view the shortcomings of others with sympathy rather than with judgment. No one of us can truly say, I am better than the next. By that same token, no one of us need fear being shown worse than the next. We are all the same human stuff, no more, no less. We all need forgiveness, we all need to forgive.

Our friend Paul of Tarsus would one day write to his followers,

> *Let this mind be in you which was also in Christ Jesus. He put on no airs, sought no fame, simply humbled himself and became obedient to the point of death.*

More and more I was taking refuge in a psalm learned during childhood days. It was now my daily prayer:

> *Search me, O God, and know my heart, try me and see if there be any wicked way in me, and lead me in the way everlasting.*

This retelling is based on Luke chapter 18 and Psalm 139.

----

28. CAST THE FIRST STONE

The School of Twelve celebrate Yom Kippur, Day of Atonement, in a fashion they could scarcely have dreamed of.

"Get ready," Jesus announced, "we are going to Jerusalem for Yom Kippur and Feast of Tabernacles!"

We arrived at the Temple early, the morning following the Day of Atonement itself. Jesus had already found a teaching spot in one of the outer courts, when we heard them approaching, a noisy bunch of local teachers, half pushing, half-dragging a woman in rumpled clothes and overall state of dishevelment.

> *We caught this woman in bed with a man who is not her husband!*

The teachers were shouting at Jesus, loud enough for everyone nearby to take notice. People began gravitating our way to check out the commotion.

*Moses' Law clearly states, she must be stoned to death.
Jesus, do you favor stoning her?*

We at once sensed a trap. Yom Kippur and the temple were hardly time or place for such a matter. These teachers were apparently trying to get Jesus to publicly advocate a break with Mosaic Law.

For the moment Jesus appeared to not even notice their interruption; he simply went on greeting acquaintances But the accusers were not to be silenced. Now Jesus bent over and began writing with his finger in the dust on the floor.

I should mention, we did have an ancient ordinance, seldom used, intended to determine the innocence or guilt of any woman suspected of adultery. A priest was to collect dust from the temple floor near the altar, mix it into holy water and make the accused woman drink. As she would drink, the priest was to recite a curse reserved for any woman found guilty —miscarriage, perhaps, or worse. Was Jesus somehow suggesting that this procedure be employed under the present circumstance? The accusers were not to be put off:

*She was right in the middle of sex with a man who
is not her husband! Give us an answer, Jesus, should
she be stoned to death?*

At this, Jesus stood up and looked the woman's accusers squarely in the eye.

*You want my opinion, and you shall have it. Which-
ever one of you has never sinned in matters of sex,
go find a big rock and be first to hurl it. The rest of
us will watch.*

With that, he bent over and went on writing in the dust.
The crowd gasped. The noisy accusers, caught off guard, blanched, and in that moment went speechless. We watched as the eldest of them slipped away into the crowd, then another and another, until the woman was left standing by herself in the clearing.

Jesus looked up, and with feigned surprise asked

Well, where have all those fine gentlemen disappeared to? Didn't anyone stay on to accuse you?

Trembling with fear and mortification, the woman shook her head,

No one, Sir.

Well, I certainly am not about to accuse you. Go back home and see that you do not sin any more.

I will not forget the look in that poor woman's eyes at that precise moment, a look of disbelief and yet of belief. For the briefest of moments she hesitated, then uttering a tiny cry, turned and fled into the crowd.

Yom Kippur, the Day of Atonement, with its elaborate ceremonies and prayers for the cleansing of priests and people, had been celebrated just the day before in these very temple courts. Today we were witnessing atonement in real time. The slate of one human being and her family was being wiped clean. She, her husband, children, neighbors, and friends were being offered a chance to redeem broken promises and spin new cords of love and fidelity.

More and more it was becoming clear to me: Law can set lofty goals and define godly conduct, but cannot by itself build trust between people or persuade them to do what is right. The Torah can *define* wrong and *encourage* right, but it cannot *prevent* wrong or *guarantee* righteousness. It takes the purifying grace of God to accomplish that. We were witnessing the grace of God at work, washing clean one soul and her web of family and friends.

Jesus never acted as judge; in fact, he refused that role when asked. He would condemn sin to the very core, but guilty sinners he would not condemn. Self-righteous accusers, yes, these he would strip of their hypocrisy, and show them up as the frauds they were. But that woman, publicly humiliated as she was by self-appointed judges, he both defended and respected. He had come to redeem broken lives, heal wounded hearts, rebuild shattered hopes, repair torn relationships, reunite separated families. God had decreed a new chance for that woman, her husband, her family — perhaps even for that male bed-partner whom society so carefully shielded from exposure or penalty.

Did the lady make good on her new chance? That I have no way of knowing, for we were never to see her again. All I have to go on is that momentary look I saw on her face as her eyes met Jesus' eyes. For myself, yes, I believe she did make good. And I believe that somehow that word of forgiveness shared with her reached out to touch many beyond. I know that it touched me.

Our friend Paul of Tarsus would one day write:

> *Let those who think that they stand take heed lest they fall. No temptation has overtaken you that is not common to all humanity. God is faithful and will not let you be tempted beyond your limit, but*

will with the temptation provide a way of escape that you may be able to endure it.

We had lived Yom Kippur. We had savored atonement.

This retelling is based on John chapter 8.

BOOK FOUR

SCHOOL

29. ROCK ON ROCK

The pace of the campaign grows intense. The Twelve, convinced now that Jesus is Israel's Messiah, are pledged to secrecy on that score. They begin a series of rallies to culminate in Jerusalem. There a price will be demanded of them.

We did not linger. Jesus was determined to get back to Galilee and then to the high mountains beyond. "We must get away from the crowds," he said. "We must have space to breathe, to think, to plan, to get closer to each other and to God." So with scarcely a pause, we passed by our familiar Lake Galilee and its little-sister-lake Huleh. Soon we were climbing the steep roadway into the Golan Heights, lofty Mount Hermon towering haughtily in the clouds above us. To such a remote site crowds would scarcely be tempted to follow.

More than ever, Jesus appeared driven by an inner compulsion, a timetable that must be met. We spent one final night in a tiny village gathering provisions, then setting out before daylight, completed the climb to our intended camp site. At the foot of a great rock-cliff, from which Jordan's headwater gushed fully-formed, we finally paused. Higher still above us, Caesar's newly completed castle-fortress could be glimpsed through the cloud cover. We were for relaxing, but Jesus was not. He could scarcely wait to unburden his heart:

Tell me, who do people say that I am?

We offered various opinions gathered from talk in the market-places:

Some say you are John the Baptist come back to life.
Others say Elijah, or another of the great prophets
— Jeremiah perhaps.

Jesus nodded and shook his head by turns. Impatiently he pressed his point:

But who do you say that I am?

Mute for the moment we looked at each other, hesitant to put into words what our hearts dared think. Suddenly Simon Peter said it for us all:

You are the Christ, Son of the living God!

Jesus was ecstatic:

Good man, Simon! No living person has taught you this, God himself has shown it to you!

He glanced upward toward the imperial fortress, its battle-ments silently declaring Rome's seemingly unassailable might. Quickly he turned toward us again:

Rock-man you are! On such rock I will build my church and the powers of hell will not overcome it!

Simon trembled, as did we all. With measured words Jesus went on:

> *I am giving you the keys to the Kingdom of Heaven. Whatever you bind on earth will be bound in Heaven; whatever you loose on earth will be loosed in Heaven.*

We were staggered, bewildered. What could he possibly mean? Was he sharing with us authority equal to his own? Was he designating us to be shapers with him of the New Israel? We sensed both the immensity and the peril of his words:

> *Do not breathe a single word of what we have been saying. This moment marks the start of our move toward Jerusalem!*

Jerusalem! The word set our hearts leaping! Jerusalem and the Kingdom! Jerusalem and ourselves officials in his royal court! We were intoxicated as much by the dream of power as by the rare mountain air. Still that dream was for but a moment as he continued solemnly:

> *I must suffer at the hands of the authorities, be put to death, then be raised.*

Peter, still euphoric from his moment of high praise, could not fathom such possibility:

> *No, not that, Jesus! Anything but that!. God's Christ must not suffer or die. God's Christ must triumph and rule!*

Jesus' blazed as he wheeled to confront Simon:

Get away from me, you Satan! Whose side are you on, the side of mortals or of God?"

We stood there stunned and silent.

If you want to go with me now, you've got to carry a cross. Whoever wants to save his life is going to lose it. Whoever loses his life for my sake is going to find it. What good would it do you to gain the world while losing your soul? What could you possibly take in trade for the very core of your being?

We went limp. This was too, too much. We ate our fish and bread with scarcely a word spoken. No one had the slightest idea where to begin.

We washed in the gushing stream, unrolled our blankets, then gathered for prayer. In the lingering crimson, Jesus asked Philip to chant the evening psalm. We listened in wonder, as the day's last light melted into the waters of the Great Sea.

O Lord, our Lord, how majestic is your name in all the earth! You whose glory above the heavens is chanted! When I consider the works of your hands, what is man that you are mindful of him and the Son of Man that you visit him? You have founded a bulwark because of your foes, to still the enemy and the avenger. O Lord, our Lord, how majestic is your name in all the earth!

This retelling is based on Mark chapter 8, Matthew chapter 16, Luke chapter 9 and Psalm 8..

----

30. ONE SMALL STEP

Misunderstandings there will be among friends and family members. Yet misunderstandings need not drive people forever apart. Jesus says, tend to rifts while they are still small.

Recall, if you will, that morning in Capernaum when first we started on the Kingdom trail. Raw recruits, we had wondered how twelve strong-minded individuals, fishermen, merchants, students, politician, banker, tax collector, such as we were, could manage to get along with each other, day in, day out, week in, week out.

Joining up with Jesus meant dramatic changes in life-style. Once fiercely independent, we were now completely dependent on each other and the uncertain generosity of people we scarcely knew. Constantly on the move, we must spend nights in barns, farmyards, strange beds, often no beds at all. Seldom would our training schedule work out as planned. In big ways and small, we were bound to step on each other's toes, hurt one another's feelings.

Well aware of our sensitivities, Jesus taught us how to deal with hurts and grievances. He recalled the psalm we had shared that day we first gathered to launch the campaign:

> *How good and pleasant it is when families live together in unity! There the Lord bestows blessing, life forevermore.*

> *We said it then, and it needs saying now: 'If we're going to be living together we ought to be some kind of family.' You know how much I depend on you Twelve. You are more than just disciples now: you are my apostles, missioners, emissaries. This school of ours, this fellowship, this assembly, this church is meant to be light for the nation, and Israel in turn, to be light for the world. How you Twelve get along is the way God wants humanity to get along.*

> *You've been praying for grace to straighten out your own lives, and that is good — "forgive us our sins" — then in the same breath you add, "as we forgive those who sin against us." Grievances there will be and hurt feelings, but grievances and hurt feelings need never keep God's people apart.*

> *When you do have hurt feelings, here is what to do: go to the brother or sister who has hurt you and say, "We have got to talk! We have got to settle this between the two of us — now, before we lose each other."*

> *I grant you, that is not easy, because you feel you are the hurt one, and it seems only fair that the one who has hurt you should come and apologize. But we are not talking about what is fair; we are talk-*

ing about what is possible through the grace of God. Don't wait for an apology, chances are, apologies will never come — time is of the essence. Get up and go! Say: "Our friendship, our marriage, our partnership" — whatever the relationship — "is more important than either my feelings or yours." Swallow your pride! Talk! Communicate! There is a chance that the other will open the door and welcome you. Remember, your friendship, your marriage, your partnership is on the line and may well be saved at this point, even strengthened. Isn't that what you really want, what you have been praying for all along?

"But," you say, "what if my brother will not listen? What if he curses me, slams the door in my face, and I leave the place feeling more miserable than when I came?"

Then I say, swallow your pride and go back once-more, only this time not by yourself. This time take along a witness, possibly two, who will plead the cause with you. Even civil courts require witnesses to establish the facts. And people usually respond decently when others are involved. Maybe that person who hurt you has been wrong; then again maybe you have been wrong. Maybe both you and he have been wrong, maybe the incident was a complete misunderstanding from the word go. Lay it all out, mutually agree to settle whatever has gone wrong, pray together, shake hands, hug if you can manage it and go on from there.

"Well and good," you say, "but what if he refuses to listen to the two or three of us, simply turns a deaf ear, what then?"

Then, I say, share the matter prayerfully with the church, your fellowship of believers. Because now more than just your own feelings are involved. What started as a minor tear in the fabric must not become a rip in the fellowship. Make that stitch in time. Consider this: the future of God's Kingdom hangs on the willingness of you two to settle your difference.

"And what if with all that, he still will not listen even to the whole church – what then?"

Then, and remember I add this only as a last resort, recognize that, for the moment at least, the breach is not to be mended. Let that person be to you as an outsider – dare I use the 't' word? — a tax collector.

Ouch! I winced at what I took to be a personal slight, but Tom jabbed his elbow into my ribs and winked. That got my blood up even more. "Rabbi," I objected, "I'm not strong enough to deal like that when I've been hurt. I'm not used to putting on my sandals and going to the one who hurt me. When I'm hurt, I've got my pride." Jesus said,

Levi, friend, you just did it! You just this moment knocked at my door and said loud and clear that you took my words to be an insult. Now I understand how you feel.

Look, l will make you a promise: I will go with you every time you do go to knock at someone's door. I will take that step along with you and stand beside you the whole time. For where two or three gather in my name, I will be there in the midst of them.

That was the substance of our training session. I think we all took it to heart.

You ask, how did I do personally from then on? How did I handle misunderstandings when they occurred? Please don't put me on the spot, and I promise not to ask you. I will say this much for myself, I honestly did try, I tried to settle things quickly and quietly, I tried to pray and act as Jesus had commanded us.

I don't suppose we can ever really know how many accept that challenge, how many are courageous enough to take that small — that giant — first step. I suspect there are more than we might at first think.

One of your poets has written:

More things are wrought by prayer than this world dreams of; therefore let thy voice rise like a fountain for me day and night.

I do believe that prayers for reconciliation among siblings and friends are being lifted to God every moment of every day. I do believe that Jesus' plan for forgiveness works. And beyond our quarreling and fallings out, as that poet went on to say:

The whole round earth is bound by gold chains unto the feet of God. *

I do believe that when our courage is weak, our Lord goes with us, to stand beside us. And we marvel to see his love casting out our fear.

This retelling is based on Matthew chapter 18.
* Alfred, Lord Tennyson, Morte d'Arthur

----

31. A MAN WHO WOULD NOT FORGIVE

The quality of mercy is not strain'd,
It droppeth as the gentle rain from heaven
Upon the place beneath. It is twice bless'd --
It blesseth him that gives and him that takes.
Tis mightiest in the mightiest; it becomes
The throned monarch better than his crown;
His scepter shows the force of temporal power,
The attribute to awe and majesty,
Wherein doth sit the dread and fear of kings;
But mercy is above this sceptered sway,
It is enthroned in the hearts of kings,
It is an attribute to God himself;
And earthly power doth then show likest God's,
When mercy seasons justice. Therefore, Jew,
Though justice be thy plea, consider this,
That in the course of justice, none of us
Should see salvation: we do pray for mercy..
(William Shakespeare, The Merchant of Venice)

I think, no place on earth is dearer to my heart than our beloved
Sea of Galilee. Day by day that lake gathers in the streams
which splash from the Golan Heights. And day by day, it sends

those waters on out again, to nourish the farms and villages of the countryside. That lake is itself alive and a bestower of life, a joy to the hearts of all.

The forgiving human heart is like that sea, itself alive and more, a bestower of life for others.

There is another lake, far to the south, which likewise drinks in the waters from the Heights, but will not let them go again. You know that sea, if fact you call it Dead. It nourishes little, its shores are corrosive salt.

The unforgiving human heart is like that sea. It gathers in but will not let go; its harvest is death.

This teaching story of Jesus' was not at all a happy one:

> *In a certain kingdom, a lord called for an audit of his treasurer's books. The man was found to be one million dollars short. The law of that land stipulated that the man be sent to prison, along with his entire family, until the missing million be made up. That is exactly what the lord ordered done.*
>
> *But the treasurer fell on his knees pleading, "Lord, have patience with me, I'll pay back every penny."*

Slim chance of that, you say, but hold on: On his bed that night, the lord was troubled by the treasurer's plight. He considered the man's bleak future – sudden poverty, his family indentured, perhaps divided forever, little prospect of ever working off so huge a debt.

Next morning, he summoned the treasurer and said, "I am canceling your entire debt. You are free and clear to start with a fresh set of books."

Praise God, you say, mercy has prevailed! Wait,
the story goes on:

> *That treasurer went back to his office. There he found
> a clerk who owed him one hundred dollars. He seized
> that clerk by the throat and demanded, "Pay me my
> hundred now – or else".*

> *Now it was that clerk's turn to fall on his knees and
> plead: "Have patience with me, Sir. With time, I'll
> make good every penny". But that treasurer would
> not listen. He had that clerk thrown into debtors'
> prison.*

> *Other servants, observing all this, were deeply dis-
> tressed. To their lord they reported: something very
> wrong is going on.*

> *The lord trembled with rage. He summoned that
> treasurer one more time and exploded in his face:
> "You miserable wretch! I forgave you all that debt
> simply because you asked me. Should you not have
> had mercy on your fellow servant as I had mercy on
> you? Guards, throw this ingrate into jail until he
> makes good the entire missing million."*

To which Jesus added:

> *That is the way God in Heaven will deal with you,
> if you do not forgive your brother from your heart.*

Pity moved that lord to forgive his treasurer when he pleaded for help. Lack of pity moved that treasurer to fail to forgive when his clerk pleaded for help.

Forgiveness from the heart — that is the key to getting along in this world: pity from the gut that considers the need of the other as one's own; deep empathy, a suffering-with, that says, "I will cancel this person's debt at my own expense."

Mercy is meant to flow and keep on flowing — down from the Heights as we plead with God for forgiveness; then out from us toward those who plead with us for pardon.

I wondered aloud to Tom, "If ever I were to go back into tax work, could I look at things in that new light? Could I learn to feel from my gut for those caravan drivers who used to curse me and spit at my sandals? Could I possibly think of them as husbands and fathers with families praying for their safe return home?

Tom did not get my point at all. "What makes you think you would ever consider going back into tax work?" was his question.

My answer: "If the Kingdom of God is not meant to work in the give-and-take of business dealings or the hard-knuckle world of neighborhood and family, then what are we really campaigning about?"

I was beginning to comprehend how wide and intricately laced is the web of human interaction, how important is the pitying heart for holding together our marriages, families, friendships, partnerships, businesses, and political associations. I was coming to realize how much I had still to learn about the whole divine-human relationship. As that poet put it:

In the course of justice, none of us should
see salvation — we do plead for mercy.

This retelling is based on Matthew chapter 18.

----

32. MAKING IT GOOD

The forgiven heart is also a grateful heart. To whatever extent it finds possible, it wants to make up for wrong done, set right what can be set right, make restitution.

Zacchaeus was an old friend of mine, though not all that close. We had trained together at the Tax School in Antioch. When graduation assignments were handed out, Zacchaeus had gone with the real estate division in Jericho, while I drew my position with the caravan section in my own hometown. Since those early days, our paths had not crossed. Now we were due to pass through Jericho on our way toward Jerusalem; by chance we two might bump into each other again.

Each day on the road we were encountering bands of Passover pilgrims streaming out of the countryside toward the capital, first by dozens, then by hundreds and then by thousands. Evenings we would camp among new and different groups. Excitement kept building, as people would crowd around for their first glimpse of Jesus, possibly to hear him preach. Our job now was simply to keep him from being overwhelmed by crowds. Organized rallies were out of the question, but at rest stops and campsites, Jesus would offer brief, impromptu talks and answer questions. Now we were hearing once more those early Kingdom parables — about God's Rule being like seed scattered across the fields or like yeast making the whole loaf rise. Most of the crowds had never heard these. "You are the light of the world!" Jesus would cry. "You are the salt of the earth!" The effect was electric, as cheers filled the evening air. But, in guarded moments, he would draw us Twelve aside for intimate talk. There he would sound a somber, disquieting note, speaking of turbulent times soon to be encountered. We could sense tension mounting with each passing day.

Now the glistening houses and markets of Jericho were coming into view. People from town were already streaming onto the road to mix with our crowd surging into town. The result was bedlam, such shouting as you have seldom heard. We tried to push our way through.

"Levi Matthew!" I was amazed to hear my own name being shouted from up above. I looked up and there he was, Zacchaeus, my old class-mate, perched on a tree limb where he could see without being shoved. I suspect he had staked out that spot well in advance.

When Jesus caught sight of us two trying to communicate in all that din, he signaled to me, "I'd like to meet that friend of yours." Then to Zacchaeus he beckoned, "Come on down, man, we'll visit your place!" Zacchaeus came slithering down, and our whole party pushed west toward Zacchaeus' luxurious house, perched high on the mountain overlooking Jericho. We shut our ears to the catcalls that local hecklers hooted after us — sneers about visiting with 'scum'; that type of insult we had heard before.

Zacchaeus at once invited in his tax-office friends and their families. For all the world, that scene took me back to my farewell feast in Capernaum. These people were all ears.

> *Happy are the poor in spirit, the humble, the peacemakers, the persecuted. Keep the Torah as God intends it be kept, sincerely from the heart. Set things right with your brother now, before time runs out. Look honestly at your own sins before trying to straighten out the sins of others. Treat others as you wish they would treat you. Love not just friends, but enemies , too.*

Jesus preached on, while Zacchaeus and his friends sat transfixed, drinking in every word. Suddenly, the man jumped to his feet and began shouting, "Count us in, Jesus, count us in!"

Jesus had not mentioned a single word about giving to the poor or restoring stolen goods. But Zacchaeus, throbbing with excitement, declared then and there his intent to do something he had never considered before: "I'm going to give half my possessions to the poor. And if I've stolen anything, (get that 'if', will you!), I'll pay back every last shekel four times over!"

Jesus beamed as he listened. Leaning toward me, he said quietly,

> *Today salvation has come to this house. These people are true children of Abraham. The Son of Man has come to seek and save the likes of them!*

We were treated royally that evening. When we finally said good-night, family members and neighbors insisted we borrow their beds. I wondered as I crawled into mine, how clean linen sheets were going to feel again. It did not take long to find out, very comfortable indeed.

Next morning, Tom and I were up early for a walk through the marketplace. We watched farmers setting up stands with produce fresh from nearby farms. Talk of the evening before was on our minds, especially Zacchaeus' determination to pay back stolen monies four times over, which far exceeded any Torah requirement. I roughly estimated from my own experience, the man would need to put his hilltop mansion up for sale and cut back drastically on the family's life style.

But the question went wider and deeper than just that: Can wrongs of the past ever be set fully right? Is there such a thing as full and fair restitution to people we have hurt, a making-good to those whose lives we may have scarred or completely ruined?

I recalled my own shady tax dealings, overcharges, bribes extorted from hundreds of different caravan drivers, most of whom I had never seen before or would never see again. They had fumed at my assessments, called me a highway robber, which I grant you I was, but eventually they had paid up. You don't complain too loudly when the Roman eagle is perched right there on the counter and you still have miles to go. It had never occurred to me when I determined to follow Jesus, that I might attempt to repay those drivers the overcharges and extortions.

Tom broadened the subject even more, "Can a person who has mentally and physically abused spouse, children, relatives or friends across, say, twenty or thirty years, ever begin to make up for those deep-seated hurts? Can they ever make adequate restitution? Can they set things back as they were in happier days?

Jesus never mentioned quotas for restitution. When he forgave or healed, he would simply say, "Go and sin no more," or, "give something to the poor." Yet we had seen over and over, when people were forgiven, they felt compelled to make things as right as they could toward those they had hurt. It was a compulsion flowing from a full heart, gratitude for the goodness of God. Their eyes had been opened to see the human misery to which they had contributed. Perhaps they could still do something about it.

Early in his career, our friend Paul of Tarsus had persecuted followers of Jesus to the point of imprisonment and stoning. When he became a believer himself, he realized he could never begin to repay the families of those victims for what he had taken from them. But he could spend his remaining days sharing news of the New Kingdom with as many new souls as possible. "I am debtor to Jews and Gentiles alike," he would say. With new believers he would counsel, "If you used to steal, don't steal any more. Instead work hard at your jobs that you may have something to give to those in need." Let God's Spirit define the boundaries of restitution and show the way. The world is full of opportunities for balancing out wrongs of the past with putting things right in the here and now.

We hurried back toward Zaccheus' place, but it was already too late for farewells. Our traveling group was already moving on the crowded road. We joined them as they were about to turn into the Jerusalem pike.

This retelling is based on Luke chapter 19.

BOOK FIVE

JERUSALEM

33. WHO WASHES MY FEET?

*Jesus enters Jerusalem to great acclaim. The eager Twelve
sense kingship within his grasp. They cannot begin to
comprehend the events which are about to engulf them.*

We did not plan that uproar at the gates of Jerusalem, nor
could we possibly have halted it had we tried. That storm arose
as if out of the earth itself. Patriotic fervor invariably ran high
at Passover time, and this year seemed ready to burst out of
control. It took but the sight of Jesus, prophet from Galilee,
riding on a spirited beast down the steep Mount of Olives to-
ward the city, to ignite the charged air. Someone began chant-
ing the psalm heard repeatedly along the Kingdom trail: *"Bless
the king who comes in the name of the Lord!"* The crowds seized
the refrain and turned it into rhythmic chant:

> *Hosanna, hosanna!*
> *Save us, Good Lord!*
> *Hosanna, hosanna!*
> *God save the king!*

Some from the crowd began gathering tree branches to festoon the parade route. Others took holiday garments from their backs to line the royal roadway.

I pushed my way through the crowd toward Jesus. To my amazement, I could see tears running down the man's cheeks. He seemed not to be hearing those cheers at all, but rather to be peering down that unseen road whose goal he could envision but we could not possibly discern. Through his tears I heard him pleading as if with the city itself, its people and rulers:

> *Jerusalem, Jerusalem, if only you could have known the things that make for your peace, but now they are hidden from your eyes. I see enemies surrounding you, erecting siege-works against your walls, slaughtering you and your children as you cower inside, leaving at the last not so much as one stone atop another — all because you did not acknowledge the time of your salvation.*

Across the Kidron Valley on rocky clearings, mounted Roman guards could be seen reining their horses uneasily, their plumed helmets and riot-gear glistening in the morning sun. Their orders from the Roman Governor left no room for trouble: "No rioting will be tolerated. Police will post detachments at all bridges and gates, and will take such action as the situation may warrant."

As the noise continued to mount, Jewish officials from the city, escorted by uniformed temple guards, came pushing through the crowd, screaming, "For God's sake, Nazarene, call this demonstration off!" To these officials Jesus shouted back, "If this crowd goes silent, the walls will keep shouting!" Meanwhile the cheering swelled the more as the crush of pilgrims heaved its way forward toward the eastern gate.

Through the gate Jesus urged his skittish mount, as far as the Temple staircase. There he halted and rushed up the long flight. Fervor took hold of him there. Glancing at the sales booths set up for business right there in the temple courtyard, he shouted, "Get this truck out of here! Would you turn my Father's house into a robber's den!" With that he started to physically knock over the money-changers' tables and yank open the stalls of animals penned there for holiday sale. Birds and beasts fled screaming and bellowing among the astonished worshipers. Not a soul tried to stop him. Temple guards produced no arrest warrants, while robed priests hesitated, caught between fear of Roman reprisal and the crowd's obvious support of Jesus. "This fool must be stopped, but not today. After Passover, when the crowds have thinned out, there will be time to act." Little could they suspect — as no more could we — that within hours, one of our own Twelve would approach them with an offer to deliver Jesus directly into their hands.

For two days more, Jesus moved unchallenged through the crowds, speaking to impromptu gatherings in the temple courtyards. Evenings, at Lazarus' home in Bethany, he spoke to us with intense feeling about times of distress not far off, times which would see not only Jerusalem devastated, but the very powers of heaven shaken. We were baffled by such talk. Was he not now poised to make his bid for power? One thing for sure: all of us were now under surveillance by both temple guards and Roman military police. Tension continued to mount.

Unknown to us, Judas had already made his move. To the temple priests in their chambers he made his offer: "How much will you pay me if I hand Jesus over to you?" The priests could scarcely believe what they were hearing, yet lost no time in bargaining: "Thirty pieces of silver." "Agreed." Then and there the silver passed hand to hand. Since Judas was in charge of our Passover arrangements, his comings and goings did not alert us, Jerusalem was his home territory.

Word circulated guardedly among us: our Seder celebration would be observed in the secure upstairs room of the home of John Mark's family. Young John Mark would be available to come and go as courier, while food would be carried in by various vendors.

As we gathered in that upper room, anticipation charged the air. Now surely we would learn from Jesus exactly what he was planning. I pushed in close to him, hoping to catch some clue, perhaps to be offered some special assignment. The others, not to be outdone, also jostled for preferred position. Not one of us gave thought to the menial task of washing feet. For security reasons, servants had been instructed to remain outside the dining room.

Jesus walked to the corner of the chamber, picked up a washbasin and water pitcher, then came back. He had removed his street tunic, and tied a large towel around his waist. Without a word, he knelt down and began to wash our feet, one by one in turn, around the room.

We were utterly chagrined. Simon drew back, "Teacher, you must never wash my feet." Jesus insisted, "Unless I do wash you, Simon, you are not my man." "Well then, not just my feet, my head and hands, too." Simon was completely flustered, as were we all, utterly humiliated. I will not forget that splash of water against my ankles.

The task completed, Jesus stood up and said,

> *You call me teacher and lord, and that is right. If I,*
> *your teacher, have washed your feet, you ought also*
> *to wash one another's feet. See, I have shown you*

how. Now do for one another as I have done for you.

Humiliated, I say, all of us were thoroughly humiliated. Yet Jesus had not humiliated us, we had humiliated ourselves. He had humbled himself by acting as our servant. There is a vast difference. Humiliation is shame brought on one's own self, whereas self-humbling is virtue sent from God to further the good of others. Jesus respected us and treated us as friends ought to be treated. He wanted us to be ready for the feast. More than just having freshened feet, he wanted us to have hearts set free from the incessant need to push self forward.

> *I give you a new commandment --Love one another*
> *as I have loved you.*

Moses had said, "Love God, love neighbor." Jesus was giving us a standard by which to measure both dimensions – "...as I have loved you.'

> *This is how people will know you are my followers:*
> *by the love you show one another.*

The Seder service went forward, psalm by psalm, scripture by scripture, prayer by prayer, course by course, through the evening hours. As the long meal ended, Jesus did something which mystified us still more He reached for a fresh loaf of bread, then offered thanks and said:

> *Share this, all of you — it is my body, given for you.*

He poured one final goblet of wine, spoke a blessing and passed it to us:

> *Share it, all of you,— my blood of the New Covenant,*
> *poured for you and many more, that sins be forgiven.*

We sensed a battle beginning. Yet who the enemy or where the battlefield, none of us could comprehend.

This retelling is based on John chapter 13, Mark chapter 14, Matthew chapter 21 and Luke chapter 19.

----

34. BETRAY ME WITH A KISS?

Judas betrays Jesus, then, in remorse, hangs himself. Is forgiveness possible for such a person, such an act?

During the Passover meal Jesus stunned us with the announcement:

One of you is going to betray me.

Such a thought was simply beyond us. Each protested loudly, "I could never do a thing like that." Simon Peter was most vehement of all. He declared, "If everybody else were to fail, I would still be loyal, I would die for you, Teacher." "Would you, friend Simon?" Jesus sighed. "This very night, before first cockcrow, you will deny three times that you so much as know me."

The Passover meal went on. We had given little thought to Judas' moving in and out of the room; he no doubt had business to transact with the food vendors. It was nearly midnight when

Jesus said, "We must go outside to pray."

We made our way toward the eastern city gate, passing late celebrants moving quietly through the streets. As we walked, Jesus grew more and more distressed. He spoke earnestly of leaving us and then coming back, insisting that his departure would be for our good. He spoke of the Prince of This World coming to challenge him. He warned of harsh times ahead for himself and for us all. Repeatedly he promised that the Holy Spirit, whom he also called Counselor, would see us through difficult days.

At the city gate we passed Roman guards who closely observed us but did not detain us. At Kidron Bridge, another military detail allowed us to pass without challenge. Moving a short distance up the western slope of the Mount of Olives, we paused before an olive grove. I could read the name Gethsemane carved into the entrance gatepost. This was an accustomed place of prayer for Jesus, close the city yet free of close surveillance.

At the orchard gate, Jesus posted eight of us, with instructions to keep watch and pray. He, with the brothers James and John plus Simon Peter would go more deeply into the grove. There, as they would tell us, Jesus fell on his face and began to cry out to God in extreme agony of soul. They could find no words to describe the pathos of his prayer.

> *Father, remove this cup from me! Yet not as I will, but as you will.*

He thanked God for having given him believing followers, and pleaded that we might be shielded from evil. He implored God to keep us together as one fellowship, just as he and the Heavenly Father were one. He pleaded that, although we would have to go on living in this world, we might be protected from the Evil One. He interceded for those who would later come to believe in him through our words, that all of us together might be bonded into one perfect fellowship, one in mind and purpose, and that the love which held him to the Father might also hold us one to another. With sweat and tears he pleaded again that God would take away the cup now pressed to his lips.

The bell from Herod's palace across the valley chimed the change of watch, as one by one we at the gate dozed off.
I tried to fight that fatigue, but simply could not keep my eyes open. When Jesus came back, he found every last one of us asleep. "Watch with me," he pleaded, "please, please! The spirit is willing but the flesh is weak." Then he went back to wrestle again in agony:

> My soul is crushed to the very point of death. Father,
> take away this bitter cup! Yet if drink it I must, then
> drink it I will — your will be done!

How can I describe our shame? When he came back to us again, we were all once more asleep. He shook us by the shoulders shouting,

> It's time! It's time! The Son of Man is betrayed into
> the hands of sinners. O God, look – look who is
> showing them the way!

A line of torches had been steadily winding up from the Kidron slope, but we had neither seen nor raised an alarm. Suddenly those torches were being thrust into our very faces. We found ourselves confronted by some two dozen uniformed temple guards well armed with swords and clubs. To our consternation, pointing them the way was our own fellow disciple Judas Iscariot.

Judas had arranged a sign by which they might identify Jesus in the dark. He stepped directly up to him, exclaiming, "Teacher!" as if delighted that the two should chance to meet at this place and hour. Then, grasping Jesus by both arms, he kissed him, right cheek and left. In that moment I heard Jesus whisper,

> *Friend, why have you come? Would you betray the*
> *Son of Man with a kiss?*

Startled wide awake, Simon Peter seized the short sword he had been concealing and lunged at the guardsman approaching him. The man recoiled, blood spurting from his ear. Jesus shouted at Simon:

> *Put that sword away! Those who take the sword die*
> *by the sword!*

His words sounded across the empty darkness of that orchard, as they would sound across centuries of history, a warning too often ignored.

The guards closed in, pinning Jesus' arms behind him, binding his wrists, then pushing him toward the orchard gate.
Jesus demanded:

> *Look, you've taken the one you came for, now let*
> *these others go free!*

He need scarcely have said that, for we all had fled for our lives deep into the grove, concealing our faces lest somehow our features be recognized and remembered. Brave, loyal, trustworthy body-guards – were we not!

I must finish Judas' story; it will take but a moment. Within hours this fellow disciple of ours would be dead by his own hand. Whatever may have possessed the man to make his miserable deal with the temple priests, I cannot say, but I do know that he quickly and deeply regretted it. When it hit home to him what he had just done, he was swept with crushing remorse. He fled back to the priests, shrieking that he had made a terrible mistake, he had identified the wrong person, the man they had taken was actually an innocent bystander. The priests sniffed: too bad, that would be Judas' problem, wouldn't it, not theirs. In utter despair now and terrified, Judas flung the silver pieces at their feet. As the coins clattered across the temple floor, he rushed to find a rope and a tree at the rim of the city refuse dump. There he looped the rope about his neck and leaped to a miserable death.

Had the man but asked for forgiveness and a fresh start, without doubt forgiveness would have been his. Jesus had never, never refused a truly penitent soul – never, never. Why did Judas, so close to the one who proclaimed heaven's grace, not ask for forgiveness? He did show that crushing remorse, yes, but he never came back to ask for forgiveness. Why, why ?

In later years our talk often turned to Judas. Had we somehow been responsible for his lost sense of direction? When suicide strikes a circle of family or friends, some invariably ask, were we somehow responsible? What could we, what should we, have done differently to prevent this tragedy? Many a time we had joked with Judas about his Judean connections; had he perhaps taken our joking the wrong way? Had we during those years together really extended to him all the warmth we could have? Such questions haunt the soul but find no answers.

Or, in counterpoint, consider the possibility of receiving back someone who has betrayed the confidentiality of friendship and then does ask for forgiveness. Can trust among friends or family members, when once violated, ever be fully restored? Can the social contract, written or unwritten, which binds families, friends, business partners, political allies — when breached through acts of deceit or infidelity — be revalidated, rewritten, so as to function as before? Can the person who has offended be welcomed back fully as friend, brother, sister, lover, spouse? Can business associations be restored so as to function effectively as before? If Judas had somehow pleaded for forgiveness and come back, would we have welcomed him back into our circle as our trusted friend? Would we have loved him as our Lord loved us — and him?

We need to ask such questions if we are serious about grasping the full dimensions of forgiveness.

I say, "Yes!" Yes by the grace of God, trust can be restored. To be sure, things will never go exactly as they once did. Circumstances will have changed and expectations will have sobered, but if forgiveness has truly flowed from the heart, then trust can be reestablished. Betrayal itself can be used by God for good, and therein is perceived the ultimate grace of Heaven. A price has been paid, a price not begrudged, paid in full with the coin of divine love.

Not every aspect of the former relationship will be restored. Full forgiveness does not demand or promise that. But it does promise that all persons involved, betrayer and betrayed alike, having learned a deeper humility, will strive to live under the New Covenant in which love begets new trust and new trust in turn begets new love.

Friend, why have you come?

----

*This retelling is based on Mark chapter 14, Matthew chapter 26
and Luke chapter 22.*

----

35. CAN A SILENT GLANCE FORGIVE ?

Trapped and paralyzed by fear, Simon Peter catches a momentary glance from Jesus. That single, silent look speaks to him more forcefully than words.

Have you ever set foot in a place you later wished you had never visited? Have you ever spoken words you later wished you had never uttered? Then you will have some idea of the extent to which Simon Peter loathed himself, that night he stood trapped in the high priest's courtyard in Jerusalem.

When the guards arrested Jesus in the olive garden, they led him by torchlight back into the city, to the chambers of Annas, high-priest emeritus. The old priest was every bit alert that Passover night as he waited impatiently for the return of the temple guard. He ordered Jesus to be arraigned before him at once, so he might size up his Galilean prisoner at close range:

> *So, you are the preacher who advocates a new Kingdom. Suppose you tell us all about that Kingdom*

and those who support you.

Jesus replied,

If I am about to be charged with some offense, I request that witnesses be called.

Such an appeal for due process gained Jesus nothing but a slap across the mouth at the hand of a court functionary; Annas was in no mood to let legal niceties stand in his way. The Sabbath was due to begin in just a few hours, and this matter must be disposed of promptly. In the adjoining High Council chamber, high priest Caiaphas was already attempting to round up as many of the seventy High Council members as could be located. Annas abruptly brought his preliminary hearing to a close, jotted a few words, handed them to a bailiff, and ordered Jesus remanded to the nearby High Council chamber for trial.

We Twelve — eleven now — caught completely off guard by Jesus' midnight arrest, had run for our lives deep into the darkness of the olive garden. Soon, however, we regrouped and followed the torch-bearing guards at a safe distance back into the city. In the shadows outside the priestly court, we conferred helplessly, bemoaning our inability to enlist a single influential supporter to intercede for Jesus. The nighttime turn of events, in absence of the cheering crowds, had rendered us powerless.

John and Peter did manage to slip inside the priestly courtyard. Here they observed the temple guardsmen, their night-time mission completed, gathering around an open-pit fire, warming themselves against the midnight chill. Peter joined the fireside huddle and warmed himself, too, keeping an eye on the doors of the Council chamber for some indication of Jesus' whereabouts and fate.

A maidservant approached the bonfire, distributing mugs of hot wine. As she served Peter, she looked full into his face and said with surprise,

> *Why, you are one of that prisoner's followers, aren't you?*

Peter quickly responded,

> *That's your little joke, lady, I don't know that Galilean.*

An hour passed. Another maid questioned Peter more searchingly than the first about his identity. Peter again vigorously denied any connection with Jesus. Now, however, his loud protests were attracting curious glances from the guardsmen at the fire. One of them, turned to look directly at Peter:

> *You must be one of that man's supporters; your Galilean brogue is giving you away.*

At that, Peter shouted:

> *You can go to hell, man! I have nothing to do with that prisoner!*

From somewhere in the distance, the cry of a rooster could be heard, announcing the imminent dawn.

That sound stabbed Peter to the quick. For the moment he was back at the Passover supper in John Mark's house, boasting he would be loyal to Jesus even to the point of death. He could hear Jesus' word of warning:

This very night, before first cockcrow, you will three times deny that you so much as know me.

He heard himself protesting:

Master, I will never, never deny you! I would rather die than that!"

Now, trembling with self-loathing, Peter wished himself anywhere but in this stupid courtyard at this accursed fire. What good was he doing his lord? Rather, what harm? Gladly he would have fled, yet he remained fixed by fear, feet cemented to the pavement on which he stood.

Presently the door of the priest's chamber swung open. Jesus, his wrists still bound, was being transferred to the High Council chamber. Peter longed desperately to rush forward, to shout out some word of support, yet dared move no muscle. He was prisoner, trapped between his own self-loathing and the questioning eyes surrounding him.

A dozen steps more would bring the prisoner to the Council chamber. Midway in that brief distance, Jesus turned to glance across the courtyard. For one fleeting moment their eyes met — Jesus' and Peter's — that was all, one momentary meeting eye-to-eye. Then the bailiff pushed his prisoner forward, the Council chamber door swung open and the two were swallowed inside.

Later, we would ask Peter what that glance of Jesus had said to him:

Was it reproach?

No! It was I who kept reproaching myself for my

stupidity.

Was Jesus somehow branding you a fool?

No! It was I calling myself stupid fool, not he. I almost wished he would have then and there shamed me to my face – coward, mindless dunce that I was.

Then tell us, man, what did that glance from Jesus say to you?

That glance somehow released me from my self-loathing. It said without words, "If these hands of mine were not bound, I would gladly reach out to embrace you, Friend Simon. Did not these hands wash those feet of yours but hours ago, and have you tried moving those feet now to get out of this place?"

With that, strength rushed again into Peter's limbs. Cautiously he edged toward the courtyard gate. No one intervened. A few quick steps more and he was outside, inhaling deep draughts of cool pre-dawn air. Along the stone pavement toward a deserted corner he fled. There he paused to let burst the flood-gate of his soul. Any passerby might have wondered, why does that strapping man stand there sobbing like a child? What could he possibly have seen to cause such outpouring of soul? Little could they guess that Simon had looked into his own soul and there seen disgrace, then looked into the face of his master and there seen grace, the redeeming grace of heaven.

Somewhere in the distance, the rooster, more confident now of the morning, crowed lustily and long. Bold streaks of color lighted the eastern sky. Tears no longer fell at Simon's feet.

One silent glance had set him free.

CAN A SILENT GLANCE FORGIVE?

This retelling is based on Mark chapter 14, Matthew chapter 26 and John chapter 18.

----

36. FATHER, FORGIVE!

Levi Matthew witnesses an act of forgiveness beside which every other act of forgiveness may be measured.

Tom and I had not the faintest clue as to the fate of Jesus in the High Council chambers, except to fear the worst. Terrified and supposing that warrants must also be out for our own arrest, we made our way in the darkness to the homes of our Jerusalem hosts. There it was almost daylight when news reached us: Jesus had, in those few intervening hours, been tried by the High Council, declared guilty and sentenced to death. He had been transferred to the imperial headquarters of Pontius Pilate, the military governor. There our priests were presenting formal charges against Jesus, demanding that the Roman general ratify their sentence of death.

Cautiously Tom and I ventured back out into the streets. As we approached the imperial court, a crowd was already gathering. We stayed well to the rear, avoiding even a nod of recognition toward the others whom we spotted in the crowd. Now we could hear the nature of the charges against Jesus being read by the Council lawyers. The charges were three in number:

1. He is a threat to Israel's national security.

2. He advocates that people not to pay the imperial tax.

3. He claims to be Christ, a king.

Pilate had misgivings about passing judgment on what he considered a local Jewish matter, yet in view of the charges implying sedition, felt compelled to conduct at least a hearing. Summoning Jesus inside his chamber, he came at once to the point -- did Jesus consider himself to be king of the Jews? Jesus replied,

Yes, I do.

Beyond that Jesus refused to utter a single word, which astonished the Roman greatly.

The priests remained outside the court to avoid ritual contamination. Pilate stepped outside to them, to announce that he had heard the case and found no crime warranting the death penalty. However, he conceded, he would have their prisoner flogged before releasing him. That, to Pilate, seemed a reasonable disposition which should satisfy the priests, whatever their motive. Roman flogging would be no pretty spectacle.

The governor had not at all anticipated the growing crowd's reaction. Now they began to shout, demanding that Jesus be crucified. Pilate found this situation hard to believe – were these Jews actually demanding that one of their own be put to Roman torture? He began to see himself as being used by the priests, but by now the cry for death was swelling into rhythmic chant, "Crucify him! Crucify him!" Pilate sensed the possibility of riot.

At this point the governor shrugged in resignation. So what was one Jew more or less to him or to Rome? He washed his hands in sight of the crowd, to establish his own innocence for the official record, then hurriedly set his initials to the death order. At once a military detail was dispatched to execute the sentence. There must be no delay, for by now the sun was fully up and the Jewish Sabbath just hours away.

I went sick to my stomach as I heard that Roman order of death read aloud.

Pilate had one petty satisfaction left: he ordered that the placard denoting Jesus' crime be worded, "Jesus of Nazareth, King of the Jews." That would remind these locals not to toy too far with Rome's decency. He shook his head in disgust and disappeared into his quarters.

Flogging must precede execution. The gates of Imperial Square were swung wide, so the crowd might both see and hear Rome's whip in motion. Thirty-nine times the lead-tipped whip whined and dug into Jesus' flesh. I could not watch, yet shuddered at the dull thud of each descending stroke.

Next came a mock coronation, the soldiers' own impromptu idea for ridiculing our people in light of the kingship charge. They threw an old purple robe across Jesus' bleeding shoulders and braced him upright in front of the flogging-post. Twisting thorn branches, they crushed these as a crown onto his head. One of them with a stick dubbed him monarch while others took turns at anointing -- spitting into his eyes. Kneeling together on the pavement, they shouted, "Hail, King of the Jews!" offering him a left-handed Roman salute, all the while splitting their sides with laughter. Thus they showed their contempt for our nation, for our holy rites, and for this stranger from Galilee called by God to save the land and someday Rome as well.

We watched our lord and master being thus humiliated. Our high dream of a new and righteous Kingdom had come to such a pathetic end.

From the imperial storeroom the execution detail procured three gibbet-beams and laid them on the shoulders of Jesus and two other prisoners sentenced to execution. The three were ordered to follow a mounted officer, who forcibly pushed a path through the Passover crowd, heading toward the city gate.

I could not believe what was happening, yet followed numbly. Women in the streets, catching sight of the spectacle, shrieked aloud. Jesus, weakened by loss of blood and the weight of that beam, collapsed onto the cobblestones. The mounted officer halted momentarily, wheeled and commandeered a man from the crowd to help Jesus carry his beam.

The site of execution was a rocky knoll outside the city wall — Skull Hill, Golgotha, Calvary, in our various local dialects. The officer dismounted, and ordered that the prisoners be laid on their backs on the ground. The troops now took the victims' arms, stretched them the width of the cross-beams and proceeded to drive spikes through the fleshy portion of their hands.

As the nails pierced their flesh, two of the condemned men screamed vile curses at their Roman tormentors. As the nails pierced Jesus' wrists, he cried out,

*Father, forgive them — they don't know what they
are doing!*

At rallies in Galilee we had heard Jesus insist over and over,
"You must not judge, you must not condemn, you must for-
give." But mind you, that was under benign circumstances.
Here, subjected to brutal torture, it seemed impossible that any
person could recall — much less want to recall — precepts like
that. Yet Jesus did! And that to me is the ultimate mystery and
majesty of the man. My own heart was being ripped to shreds,
and it seemed that every vestige of human decency was being
violated, yet here he was lifting up the banner of mercy and
forgiveness.

Were these tormentors really unaware of what they were do-
ing? Of course not. They were aware, every last one of them.
They were promoting national security and at the same time
protecting their own backsides. Pilate understood what he was
doing: he was maintaining Roman law and order, while mak-
ing sure of his own political standing with the emperor; three
more troublesome Jews were being eliminated. The Roman
troops understood what they were doing: they were carrying
out military orders and earning points on their charts toward
home-leave; hammering spikes through prisoners' wrists just
happened to be part of the whole dirty business. The priests
understood what they were doing: they were using Rome itself
to get rid of a heretical Galilean who had threatened their au-
thority as custodians of true religion.

And yet not one of them understood. Not one realized that
they were undermining the very foundation of righteous law,
national security, and true religion. Jesus of Nazareth, nailed
alive to that wood, understood and believed. In that moment
of excruciating torment and shame, he was crying,

Father, forgive them!

The crossbeams, their living burdens dangling, were hoisted atop their posts and into their sockets. More spikes were now driven through the prisoners' ankles to prevent too quick a suffocation. Crucifixion must drag on for full effect. Tom and I watched from a distance, unable to utter a word. It was too much to take in, too much to tell.

In one of your news journals, an eminent essayist recalls one of the hideous national crimes of your own times, in which six million of my countrymen were declared enemies of the state and systematically subjected to slave labor, torture, and death. This essayist wrote:

> *The Holocaust not only lies beyond compensation; it*
> *also lies beyond explanation, reconciliation, sentiment,*
> *forgiveness, redemption or any of the mechanisms by*
> *which people attempt to set wrong things right.* *

Jesus did not believe as that earnest essayist believed at his moment of writing. Jesus prayed, "Father, forgive them, they do not understand what they are doing," convinced that, however heinous the offense, however brutal the means, redemption was possible, reconciliation was possible. What if he had believed otherwise — that his tormentors were beyond the bounds of salvation? What if he had believed that you and I are doomed by our own sins to remain outside the pale of God's forgiveness?

Jesus believed that one day by the grace of Heaven, all of us, however vile our hatreds, however warped our understanding of right, however abject our surrender to the pressures of position, might yet be drawn within the circumference of God's grace. He was giving himself to death in that faith.

Father, forgive.

This retelling is based on Luke chapter 23.
* Roger Rosenblatt, Time Essay "Paying for Auschwitz",
Time, April 12, 1999

----

37. REMEMBER ME!

It was perhaps the slowest and cruelest form of torture ever devised by the human mind — crucifixion. The victim's body cried incessantly for relief but, by intent, no relief was allowed. For Rome this was the ultimate medium of persuasion: victims made to suffer in full, naked view of the populace for a second or even a third day – as, ever so slowly, body vitality drained away. Let the sight of a crucifixion in progress be grim warning to any potential rebel: do not so much as think about questioning the authority of Rome.

We dared venture no closer than the edges of the scene, fearful lest someone, Roman or Jew, might suspect our connection to Jesus. Nor did we linger more than moments at a time. Through the course of those hours, Tom and I left and returned a dozen times. We sought out the home of Nicodemus, a sympathetic Council member, who had not been part of the nighttime trial, and had not voted in the dawn session that condemned him. Nicodemus, however, was not to be found.

At the site of the hanging, we watched Passover visitors moving in and out of the city. They would pause for a moment,

shake their heads in dismay, then hurry on, hoping to come
on happier scenes. Temple leaders stopped as well, display-
ing grim satisfaction at what they had accomplished. Looking
up at the victim on the center cross, they shook their fists and
shouted, "So you are our Christ, well, show us your credentials,
man; let's see your friends come rescue you from this Roman
orchard." The soldiers at first joined the sarcastic jesting, but
soon turned to other pursuits, throwing dice for the victims'
belongings, thus passing the hours. Everything we considered
holy was being subjected to ridicule and scorn.

One of the thieves hanging there, joined the ridicule: "Hey,
Christ, why don't you spring the lot of us free? Call up your
reserves." Tom and I winced for shame. We were his reserves, a
shameful, powerless bunch of cowards, hiding in the shadows,
afraid even to let our faces be seen and noted.

The condemned man on the far cross remained silent. I cannot
tell you that man's name; some have called him Dysmas, let
that do. Dysmas called to the other, "Cut your sarcasm, man!
Don't you have a shred of decency left? We're getting what
we've got coming; this fellow has committed no crime." With
huge effort he swung his body toward the one hanging near
him. The placard on Jesus' cross read: "King of the Jews." I do
not know how Dysmas may have understood those words, but
I did hear him whisper hoarsely,

> Jesus, remember me when you come in your kingly
> power.

That request seemed absurd in the light of it all — one man,
himself condemned and dying, asking another, likewise con-
demned and dying, for such a preposterous favor. I flashed
back to that day when James and John, sons of Zebedee, had
requested a similarly preposterous favor: when the Kingdom

would be established, might they be designated as top officials, one to sit at Jesus' right hand, the other at his left. Jesus had replied that these positions would be filled by persons designated at the appropriate time by the Father in Heaven; his own calling was to serve and offer his life a ransom for many. Now our king hung bound and dying on a Roman cross. At his right hand and left hung two thieves, defilers of the laws of God and man. One of them was pleading to be remembered when the Kingdom should come.

I caught a glimpse of Jesus' face in that moment. Once again, he seemed to be looking down that road whose goal he could envision but we could not possibly discern. "Friend," I heard him say,

> *I tell you in truth: before this day is done, you will be with me in Paradise.*

Tell me, good reader, can a life wasted across the years be redeemed in its final moments? Is there such a thing as genuine repentance when one is faced with imminent death? Should latecomers who have long disregarded God and holy things be offered Heaven's grace on equal terms with those who have persevered across long years? What do you think?

Jesus had often told a story about a vineyard owner who hired workers at various hours during the same working-day, almost up to quitting time. Each worker at the moment of hiring agreed to the wage of one dollar. At quitting time each received that exact amount – one dollar. Those who had labored through the noontime heat complained, "Unfair!" But the owner insisted, was it not his right to pay late-comers the same as the all-day crew? God is fair by God's standard, and God's standard assures unstinted grace for every sinner who turns back home.

To Dysmas, at the point of death, Jesus said, "Before day's end, you will be with me." That I do believe. I do believe that every child who, though having wandered foolishly or far, at the last returns ragged and barefoot to confess, will find the Father's waiting arms.

Something more haunted my thought: Suppose that at that extreme moment, someone *had* in fact come rushing in to rescue Dysmas from his gibbet, would there have been anyone then to remember him and welcome him back into functioning society? Would there have been friends waiting to wish him a fresh start – help him rethink, retrain, retool, take up some new and useful occupation? I am told that in your day, a number of chapels built inside prison walls carry the name 'Church of Saint Dysmas'. That is a small signpost toward redemption. But do you also have churches outside prison walls that offer wider hope, and devote their energies to helping ex-offenders find a new and better way? That would be a true sign of acceptance for the prodigal brother or sister come home.

My thoughts were jolted back to reality. The sky was turning inky black as stifling air closed in, surely it must storm. People drew their wraps more closely about them and quickened their pace toward the city gates. Jesus, now in terrible agony, pleaded,

> *God, my God, why have you forsaken me? Why do*
> *you stay so far away? Do you not hear the sound of*
> *my groaning?*

Many another sufferer across the ages had cried from the depths those same woeful words, yet never, I think, so piteously as I heard them wrung from his lips that awful afternoon.

Desperately I wanted to rush forward, to speak to him, to embrace him, yet fear fixed me to the spot on which I stood. I wished to God then, that I, too, might die with him.

Presently Jesus lifted his shoulders for one final shout, this time not the cry of a sufferer at all, but more the cry of a victor on a battlefield exulting that the conflict has been fought through and won.

Then silence fell across the knoll. For an unmeasured moment no one moved.

Then I heard him quietly say,

> *Father, into your hands I yield my spirit.*

And he died.

This retelling is based on Mark chapter 15, Luke chapter 23,
Matthew chapter 27 and John chapter 19.

THE INN:
The Green Cathedral

Our week was winding to a close. Levi Matthew announced free-time for the remainder of the afternoon. Following that, Henri would be serving early supper — please answer his bell promptly! — and then the final series of stories would get underway. For Abby and me this short break offered chance to search out the Green Cathedral. Not a difficult search, Kori assured us, we would find the place a short half-mile below the Inn in a small glade where deciduous trees had room to breathe. For Kori, the cathedral was a project of love still much in progress. Though far from finished, it was open for prayer or meditation.

Kori had been hauling dozens of young aspens into the clearing and re-planting them evenly-spaced, so as to form an enclosure somewhat longer than wide. An opening at the back as we approached was obviously intended as entrance; branches at the far end were being espaliered to form a window looking toward the tall cedars beyond. The young trees would eventually reach their tops across to form a vaulting roof, but for that would need more years. For furnishings, Kori had constructed a few simple wooden benches resting on rocks gathered from the glade, that was all. At the entrance he had posted a small, wooden, hand-lettered tablet:

I know a green cathedral,
A hallowed forest shrine,
Where leaves in love join hands above
And arch your prayer and mine.
(Carl Hahn 1921)

We approached the cathedral hand in hand, without saying a word. But my thoughts had been racing; I had made up my mind, I am going to spill it to Abby — my mixed up inside. Yes, we do have our agreement about soiled linen kept strictly out of sight. But my past is eating away at my present, and my present is worried sick about our future, and I am going plain berserk. I must get this off my chest, and Abby has got to understand.

We entered the cathedral silently and found one of the benches. As our eyes took in the place, I gathered a deep breath, summoning up courage to begin, then cleared my throat.

Sensing that, Abby quickly lifted a finger and pressed it to my lips -- "Shhh." I was startled and turned to look directly at her. There was a glow in her eyes I could not recall having seen before. She began:

"There is something I've got to say to you before I explode!

"Do you remember that song in 'Superstar', where Mary Magdalene wonders, 'In these past few days when I've seen myself, I seem like someone else?' That's been happening! That's been happening to me!

"When we first started listening to all those stories back there, I said they could not possibly have anything to do with the years I had gone through with Brad. But then, suddenly the old hurts started creeping back – not the physical abuse so much as the deep disappointments, our inability to resolve any problems together, the nights I had to wonder was he ever coming home, and his condition when he did finally did come in. I know it takes two to make a marriage and two to break one, and I am a long way from perfect, but I was trying. God knows, I was trying. And I think, in his own way, Brad was trying, too, but everything just got worse.

"Do you have any idea what I'm trying to say? Do you?

"You and I made our agreement: don't ask, don't tell; and here I am spilling my guts anyway. But I can't keep it in, because . . . because . . . suddenly I was hearing those stories say something that I had not been hearing before, and that something was changing everything.

"I think it was the stories about those two women who were handed such raw deals from those guys — that one woman who cried beside Jesus' feet and poured her perfume over them. And then the one who got dragged into the temple court after being caught in bed with some strange creep. I could feel for those two women — not for what they were doing, but for the way they were getting hurt by people who couldn't understand them and took advantage of them. They were scared skinny, both of them, and then the way Jesus stood up for them, and they walked away with their heads held high. I said, 'That is what I've been waiting to hear — that God is listening, and I can find the courage to make a second marriage go — our marriage, yours and mine.' And I began to cry. I tried to not let you see, but I knew you could see by my face that I'd been crying.

"Because I suddenly realized, that is the point of it all —the point of that whole bunch of stories we've been listening to, the whole shebang. God has been trying to work things out for people, bring them back to himself and to each other! Like that wasteful kid coming home broke after he'd messed up his whole life, trying to find the right words to say to his dad, and the father says, 'Don't you know, boy, I've been listening to you all along, I was out there with you, and now it's just time to invite the neighbors over, call in the fiddlers, and roast that beef that we've been fattening up. We're not stone broke, you know.'

"I'm those two women, I'm that boy, I tell you, I'm somebody else! I'm a baby yelling for more milk! And I'm not afraid any more that our marriage isn't going to work, because now I trust myself, and I trust you, and I trust God as I never thought I could again!"

With that Abby simply went to pieces, crumpled into my arms, there on that wooden bench, sobbing with her whole body. Then, when she finally looked up at me, she was laughing instead, laughing with her whole body, crying and laughing at the same time.

When Abby had started into all this, I was shocked. If I had any thought of unloading my own problems, that was gone. She was astonishing me more and more with every sentence, and I could not be sure whether I was actually hearing her or not. Then all of a sudden, the dam inside me broke, and there I was crying and laughing along with her. Our souls were melting, melting in that moment into each other. There in that green cathedral our souls were becoming one, and our prayers were reaching upward toward heaven like the branches of those brave little aspen trees. I finally did find one word to murmur over and over:

Thank you! Thank you, God! Thank you, Abby!
Thank you, Levi Matthew and you other guys,
back there at the Inn!

Henri's bell was clanging like mad in the distance. He had warned, don't be late for supper.

Sorry, Monsieur Chef, you did not think to call in fiddlers, did you? Well, do you suppose you are going to tempt Abby and me now with just your veal roast?

BOOK SIX

WORLD

38. RE-EXPLORING THE KINGDOM

The Eleven lie stunned and dazed. How could the King-dom plans have gone so wrong? Within a single day Jesus has been betrayed, seized, executed and buried. How could they even begin to dream of the events now about to en-gulf them?.

We were as living dead, numbed beyond description by grief and shame. I cannot describe to you the depth of our depression. Jesus was no more. We had witnessed his last hours, heard his last words. Through it, we had not raised one finger to help him or uttered one word in his defense.

Two Jewish High Council members, Nicodemus and Joseph, until now cautious supporters of the Kingdom, came forward boldly to claim Jesus' body from the Romans. Three women from the group who had traveled with us from Galilee helped wrap the corpse in a linen shroud and lay it in a nearby rock grave. The arrival of the Sabbath curfew prevented further embalming. A Roman guard was posted to forestall possible tampering at the grave site.

Shrouded in misery and bitterness, daring hardly to speak or even look at each other, we Eleven crept to our hosts' homes. There we spent two wretched, sleepless nights and the hours of that horrible Sabbath — a day of rest which brought no rest, but only unending waves of misery, guilt and self-recrimination. We had failed our lord in every respect. When he needed us most, we had thought only to save ourselves.

As the Sabbath sun went down, the new week began and shops reopened. The Galilean women who helped with the burial now purchased spices with which to complete the embalming. Dawn found them already on their way to the grave-site. We Eleven made our way, one by one, to John Mark's home, where we had eaten the Passover supper with Jesus.

As we arrived, astonishing reports greeted us. From one Galilean woman, then from another, came word that they had seen Jesus alive and that he had spoken with them. That obviously was not to be believed, such dreams were a figment of their own wishful thinking. With my own eyes I had seen Jesus unquestionably dead, his corpse laid away in that rock tomb. Yet our astonishment grew out of bounds when Simon Peter burst in to shout that he, too, had seen Jesus alive!

I cannot describe for you the ecstasy that overwhelmed us all that evening, when, huddled as we were behind bolted doors, we suddenly saw Jesus there in our midst! My heart fairly leaped from my body to see him alive, healthy, radiant, vibrant! This was the same Jesus we had known and traveled with, yet somehow this was a new and different Jesus, resplendent as we had not known him before!

Shalom!

His booming greeting, shook my whole body and re-charged my soul. "Shalom, it means a thousand things," so you sing. To me in that moment, his Shalom meant everything: forgiveness, renewal, another chance at life. My broken spirit soared. We heard him say, "I will meet you in Galilee," and with that he was gone from our sight.

I cannot describe to you the impulse that powered our feet, the fire that drove our souls, as we covered those miles back to Capernaum. I cannot tell you how I trembled when Jesus gathered us once more to breathe on us the promise of the Holy Spirit. I cannot tell you my thrill at climbing once again with him to that campsite on the Golan Heights – there where the waters of the Jordan gush fresh from the cliff-side to nourish the land. At this very spot we had confessed him to be Israel's Messiah. Here he had unnerved us, declaring that he must suffer and die in Jerusalem, then be raised to new life.

On that mountain height, time stood still. How long we were with him I cannot say – a fortnight, I suspect. Our training sessions, so often cut short along the earlier campaign trail, received undivided attention now. Those many irksome interruptions — Jesus' constant changing plans to respond to people's pleas for healing, delays as he became involved in their problems, his unwillingness to turn away mothers bringing children for blessing, his constant attention to people's misfortunes — all these had not been time wasted, energy diverted from our intended schooling. These had been the very essence of the Kingdom taking shape before our eyes. *Those interruptions of mercy were the Kingdom in motion!* He had been traveling on that road whose goal he could envision but we could not possibly discern.

The Kingdom had not been shattered at all, as we supposed and feared. He had endured a mighty battle, a battle fought through to the end! He had faced the forces of evil and defeated them before our very eyes. He had wrested humanity free. Even as we had stood wringing our hands in despair, he was crying thanksgiving to God that the battle was done!

Suddenly the whole campaign became clear. We could appreciate his having wrestled with Satan in the desert: his having renounced riches, fame and power to follow the Way of the Suffering Servant, his having reached out to outcastes like me and my kind with hope and salvation. Now we could understand his short temper when he called his friend Simon Peter "Satan." He himself had been tempted like us. Tempted but never to the point of giving in. And when that final bitter cup of sorrow was pressed to his lips, he had drunk it to the dregs. He had seen God's will done to the end, and God was declaring him King and Lord of All. Now he could boldly say:

All power is given to me in heaven and on earth!

True, the leaders in our land had rejected him, had considered him and the Kingdom a threat to themselves, a dishonor to God. Yet, by no means were those leaders beyond the scope of salvation. Caiaphas and his fellow priests who condemned him as heretic were not enemies, they were sinful human beings for whose redemption he had prayed. Pilate, the Roman who signed his death warrant, was not an enemy; he was a sinful human being for whom he had shown respect.

The satanic forces which had enslaved these leaders, and which enslave all humanity, these were the ultimate foes. These Jesus had faced, and these he had beaten. And his victory now was for anyone pleading God's mercy. We were being commissioned to announce that news, to proclaim that victory. Now was the redemption of humanity, now the forgiveness, now the atonement, now the wiping clean of the slate, now the dawn of the age of righteousness and peace.

Share this news!
Teach the nations!
Baptize them!

On these very heights, Jesus had given us the keys of
the Kingdom. Suddenly that commission was coming clear.
The Holy Spirit would fill us with wisdom to distinguish right
from wrong within the unfolding processes of history. The
Torah could be understood as God intended: "Love the Lord
your God, love neighbor as yourself," twin streams of divine
revelation, like the early rains and late, blessing our land and
nations beyond. "Love as I have loved you," would draw to-
gether again souls torn apart by human frailty.

Jesus glanced upward toward the citadel looming on Hermon's
brow; somehow its battlements seemed less threatening now.
He looked toward the Great Western Sea, highway to lands un-
known; somehow, far-off nations seemed accessible now, their
peoples no longer alien. He nodded toward the mountain pass-
es to the East, beyond which lived our scattered cousins, and
farther still, a multitude of tribes unknown to us now but one
day to be called family. All these might somehow be reached
for God. Here was a world waiting to be linked as one, drawn
together by the love of the Almighty and love among siblings.
Walls of prejudice would fall now. No people are foreign, no
race unclean, all are God's children, chosen and free.

Teach them. Baptize them in the name of the Father,
Son, and Spirit. You will not go alone. My Spirit
will empower you. I will be with you to the close of
the age!

What day or hour we finally broke camp, I cannot tell you.
As we descended the heights, we could see pilgrims streaming
southward toward Jerusalem, there to celebrate the Early Har-

vest. Presently we would join them. Soon the Kingdom would find fulfillment.

This retelling is based on Mark chapter 16, Matthew chapter 28, Luke chapter 24, John chapter 20.

----

39. WALLS COME TUMBLIN' DOWN

Joshua fit d' battle ob Jericho,
An' d' walls come tumblin' down.
(traditional)

Simon Peter was guest in the home of a friend on the Mediterranean seacoast. There he dreamed a troubling dream. Down from the sky came a great sheet loaded with all sorts of animals, creatures designated by the Torah as unclean — pigs, camels, hares and such — meat strictly forbidden for us to eat. A voice said, "Get up, Peter, slaughter and have lunch." Peter objected, "That I cannot do! No non- kosher food has ever entered my mouth." The voice went on, "Don't you call unclean what God has made clean." Three times in quick succession that same dream occurred.

Simon was startled wide awake by a knock at the door. There stood three Roman soldiers, on orders, so they explained, from their commander, one Captain Cornelius of the Roman Syrian occupational forces: "The Captain wishes to invite Simon Peter to visit him at his home." Struck by the coincidence of that extraordinary dream and this most unusual invitation, Simon Peter gathered his traveling companions and rode off with the Roman escort.

At the gate of the Gentile compound, Peter halted and dismounted uneasily. Never in all his days had he set foot inside a Gentile home. Silently and deeply he breathed a prayer, then crossed the Roman threshold:

> *One small step for a man.*

The captain came running forward and was about to kneel, but Peter objected:

> *Sir, you are looking at a mere human like yourself!*
> *But I must tell you, what I am doing here is strictly*
> *against Jewish law: I ought not be entering the home*
> *of a Gentile. Still God has persuaded me, I must no*
> *longer consider any person or race unclean.*

The captain had assembled his entire household: family members, military aides, civilian staff, servants. All were waiting for Peter to tell his story.

> *I am a devout Jew, but God has made clear to me*
> *that heaven plays no favorites among races. In any*
> *nation anyone who fears God and does what is right*
> *is acceptable to him. Let me share with you, then,*
> *the news I am privileged to share among my own*
> *countrymen.*

With that, Simon launched into his story of Jesus' ministry — his preaching, his healings, his arrest by the Jerusalem authorities, his sudden death at the hand of the Roman procurator, his being raised to life again by the power of God. For a moment Simon paused, then went on:

> *We spent time with Jesus after he rose from the dead. He commanded us to announce that God has declared him judge of everyone, living or dead. Our great prophets also bear witness to Jesus, promising that those who believe in him will experience forgiveness of sins through his name.*

Peter had got this far, when a sudden wave of emotion swept over that gathering. The air fairly exploded as the Holy Spirit came over Cornelius and his household. This enclave of Roman expatriates found themselves weaving, waving, speaking to one another in ecstatic tongues.

Peter's traveling companions were thunder-struck to see Gentile people thus overcome by the Spirit. Peter shouted, "Water! Someone, bring water!" Whereupon, those Gentile people, old and young alike, were baptized by Peter, just as, back at Jerusalem, Jewish believers were being baptized.

News of this seemingly flagrant breach of Torah law, this fraternizing with Gentiles, traveled as by wind back to our Jerusalem community. No sooner had Simon and his party returned home, than he was called on by some to answer: Had he intentionally set foot inside a Roman home? Had he knowingly and willingly eaten Gentile food at a Gentile table? Peter related, detail by detail, the entire incident: his dream, the invitation from Cornelius, his warm reception in the Roman villa, the outpouring of the Holy Spirit, the baptisms:

> *If God was giving these Romans the same gifts he had given us, who was I to attempt to restrain the*

hand of God?

Day by day the Spirit was challenging our thinking, bending our traditions, stretching our views. Walls of separation that had stood a thousand years, barriers long considered as having been set in place by God himself, were suddenly crumbling at the Spirit's bidding. We were looking down a new and untried road. Could this be the road down which Jesus himself had so often looked, whose goal he could see, but we had been unable to discern?

One day, our friend Paul of Tarsus would write:

> *Christ is our peacemaker. He has broken down the dividing wall of hostility, those restrictions that kept us apart, and has made of Jew and Gentile a single new humanity. Now we approach God together in one Holy Spirit, laboring side by side as fellow citizens to complete a mighty building project — a temple of humanity totally dedicated to God.*

A temple of humanity totally dedicated to God! As we took seriously the command of Jesus to go to all of the world, we were being made again and again to re-examine our attitudes concerning race, culture and religious practice. Like the prophets of old, we were being overwhelmed by the vastness God's grace. Invincible Rome itself was starting to feel the prevailing presence of Jesus, not by might or by power, but by the Spirit of the Lord. We recalled how Jesus had said, if we would stay with him, we would be given a whole new concept of who is enemy and who is friend. With Peter we had taken

One small step for a man, one giant leap for humanity!

This retelling is based on Acts of the Apostles chapter 10.

----

40. RECONCILED

"The Inn of Friendships Renewed" is nowhere to be found in the Bible. We simply imagine the place into being, as earlier on, we imagined that humble home where Seth and Sarah with their children sang and lived out the psalms of the land.

The final writings of the New Testament (as with the Psalms) are not presented in story form, instead they come as letters, correspondence, written at various times and places by a variety of early church leaders, addressed to friends and congregations at various locations around the Mediterranean world. Each has a powerful note of forgiveness that we must not miss. That Simon Peter, Paul of Tarsus and James of Jerusalem might, over a period of time, have visited such an inn is not completely beyond the realm of possibility. So, the great hearth at the Inn will serve as platform for these leaders to share their deep concerns, while the front desk will offer Levi Matthew space to complete his imaginary journal.

It was Tom's suggestion that he and I head for Persia. For

years we had been preaching the Gospel as a team, town-by-town across Israel and in nearby provinces. Yet never had Jesus' words of commission stopped ringing in our ears:

> . . . *Jerusalem, Judea, Samaria, and the farthest*
> *corners of the earth.*

"We should be following Alexander's route to the East," Tom kept insisting. "The general pushed his armies deep into Persia and beyond, believing that through conquest he could unite the world. Our mission is a surer one – to save the world with a new birth of the spirit. Those far-off nations are still waiting to hear the Gospel."

So, we set about preparing for a journey from which we might never return. Months were spent in learning all we could about lands to the east with their peoples and languages, locating interpreters, buying camels for the desert trek, stocking up on provisions to last through the journey.

We should never have loaded ourselves down with that much gear. On the earlier Kingdom campaign trail, Jesus had always said, "Take only what you'll need for today, no more; after that let listeners supply your needs." We had forgotten that advice, and so started toward Syria carrying far too much. Halfway to Damascus we were set on by bandits out of the high hills, who in one devastating swoop clubbed us to the ground and made off with it all — camels, provisions, everything. Everyone in our party except me came through with no more than cuts and bruises, but when I was knocked from my camel, I suffered both legs badly broken.

I had no choice but to be carried back to Israel for recuperation. We agreed that Tom should go on ahead, while I would rejoin him whenever my poor legs would permit. Thus, on sudden notice, we reached our sad moment of parting, good brother Tom and I. Together we had labored long. Deep in my heart I suspected that I was never to see him again. He did send messages faithfully from Persia where he met thousands of devout Hebrews anxious to hear the Gospel message. Endlessly restless, he continued on, refusing to stop until he had retraced Alexander's entire route clear to India. Then, abruptly, his letters stopped coming. How he fared among the Gentiles of India, I was never to learn but could only surmise.

For me this turn of events meant one more adjustment of career. From Roman tax collector, to disciple in Jesus' school, to mission preacher across Israel, I had always been able to more or less chart my own life. Now, through this blow of fortune, I found myself in daily need of the ministry of others. Like father Israel at the Brook Jabbok, I had to plead with God each morning for courage to go on — also, like father Israel, I was to limp, as you see, for the remainder of my days.

It was in the town of Shechem, while recuperating, that I discovered the Inn. Shechem, like Capernaum, is a crossroads town, rich in the lore of our people. There I learned to know Malachi, the aged innkeeper, and shared with him the good news of Jesus. Soon Malachi confided that he wanted to donate his inn to the Christian cause; would I possibly stay on to manage it? My first reaction was to say no; but the more I considered, the more I came to appreciate, here the world was day by day coming to my door. This great hearth could become my pulpit, these travelers my ever-changing congregation. I accepted Malachi's offer with a growing sense of excitement.

The signpost at the roadside must be re-carved to read: "The Inn of Friendships Renewed." Here walls of prejudice and misunderstanding would fall as God's love for friend and stranger alike would be shared. Here, human hearts separated by circumstance, would be re-bonded with cords of divine forgiveness. And that, by the grace of God, is what I lived to see happen. Day by day, week by week, countless business travelers on assignment, Seths and Sarahs with their children, soldiers, royal emissaries, would stop for rest and renewal. Worn by the miles and many another burden, they would gather with me when the evening meal was finished to hear my stories of times spent with Jesus on the road: How poor and anxious people had rejoiced to hear his promise of a new Kingdom. How our rulers had handed him over to the Romans for execution, yet how God had raised him to life again, defeating the very powers that hold human souls captive. Day by day guests would depart the Inn for distant destinations filled with new hope and resolution, their heads held high, their spirits soaring.

<u>Simon Peter</u>

It was a happy day when old friend Simon Peter stopped at the Inn! I had always admired that man and readily accepted his leadership among our Twelve. The fire in Simon's eye was flashing as brightly as ever when he arrived to spend a short week. He could stay just long enough to compose urgent letters.

"Those new churches burn in my heart," Peter said, "New believers are paying dearly to profess Jesus as Lord. Their homes are being confiscated, their civil rights taken away, some serve jail sentences, some suffer death by burning at the stake. I am writing to these congregations to say:

> *Hang in there, good people! Don't let persecution deter you from becoming all that God has called you to be! Remember, gold has to be purified by smelting, and you are being smelted, so to speak, for the purifying of your souls.*

> *Remember that Jesus suffered not for wrongs of his*

own. He was not guilty of sinning or lying. When he was insulted, he did not hurl insults back. He simply placed his cause into the hands of God. He carried our sins to that tree so that we might be made alive to better things.

You followers of Christ have become a Holy Nation, a Royal Priesthood, a Chosen Race. Now show forth the goodness of God who has called you out of darkness into his marvelous light.

If you do what is right and are made to suffer for that, you are fulfilling your calling, you are following in the footsteps of Jesus.

So, keep your consciences clear. Love one another fervently from your heart. Stay humble. Cast your care on God, and God will take care of you. Above all, hold unfailing your love for one another, since love covers over a multitude of sins.

More and more I was coming to feel oneness with the many new believers of the world. The gospel was transforming lives wherever it was spoken, and those who heard were becoming light for the world, salt for the earth in the places where they lived. Though dressed variously in the costumes of their cultures, they were alike putting on the humble yoke of Jesus.

I felt closer to Simon and his family than I had ever felt before. Closer also to those distant, unmet friends whose sacrifices were making my own troubles seem small. As Simon bade us farewell, my heart went with him.

Paul of Tarsus

From his physical appearance, you might not have called Paul of Tarsus a mighty man, but I assure you, in spirit and drive he was mighty and more, a missionary from the word go. During his brief visit, he remained ever on the alert, listening for some possible new command of the Spirit to which he must respond, right now.

Paul had gone on mission expeditions to found new congregations in Western Asia, then in Greece. These new churches had become mixed assemblies of Jews and Gentiles. Now, as he arrived at the Inn, I could see the marks which over the years physical hardship had taken on the man. He had been repeatedly beaten, starved, flogged, stoned to the point of death. Such misfortunes, he insisted, had only confirmed his determination to work harder for the cause; beatings he could endure, so long as they opened for him new opportunities for sharing the Gospel of Jesus.

At the Inn Paul would stay only overnight, then must be on his way to Jerusalem. We gathered around the hearth as he began:

> *In Christ we have become completely new people.*
> *God has reconciled us to himself, not keeping track*
> *of past wrongs. You used to be strangers, enemies of*
> *God, but God has brought you back through Jesus,*
> *to present you holy and blameless before himself.*
> *Now you and God are friends once more.*

"That is what I keep telling people, Jews and Gentiles alike; and that is what, deep-down, they are waiting to hear. Their former gods they gladly set aside, as they come to recognize the One Lord God and Father of all. They see themselves drawn into Abraham's covenant and speak of themselves as brothers and sisters with us by faith."

"But what about the Torah?" I wanted to know. "These many cultures differ so drastically from our own Jewish ways."

"They hear as their ears and the Holy Spirit allow them to hear. The big, bold Ten Commandments always stand up front. Beyond that, the Holy Spirit helps people work out laws for living together in each place, as they did at Antioch and elsewhere. To all, whatever their folkways, I say:

Get rid of anger, wrath, malice, slander, foul talk. Do not lie to each other. Remember, you have shed your old selves and been changed into something new, constantly being recreated after the image of our Creator. Here there cannot be Greek and Jew, circumcised and uncircumcised, barbarian, Scythian, slave, free-man; instead Christ is all and in all.

So, as God's holy, chosen, well-loved children, dress yourself in compassion, kindness, lowliness, meekness, and patience. Put up with one another and if one has a complaint against another, forgive the other; just as the Lord has forgiven you, that is the way you also must forgive. Above all these, put on love, love which binds everything together in perfect harmony. And let the peace of Christ rule in your hearts to which indeed you were called as members of the one body.

Are you being persecuted? Bless those who persecute you, never curse them. Live in harmony with one another. Never be haughty, but associate with the lowly; never become conceited. Insofar as it depends on you, live peaceably with everybody. Leave vengeance to God. No, if your enemy is hungry feed him, if he is thirsty give him drink; that is the way to heap

*burning coals on his head. Do not be overcome by
evil, but overcome evil with good.*

We listened, talked, and prayed together late into the night. At
dawn Paul was already dressed and ready to be on the road.
Friends kept warning, "We sense trouble ahead for you in Jeru-
salem." Paul only shrugged; for him trouble would be nothing
new.

James, Brother of Our Lord

Day by day the rumblings were coming closer, the rumblings
of war. The Sicari, a militant group in Israel, were stirring peo-
ple to rebel against Rome — against Rome, mind you! — the
mouse making bold to taunt the lion! "No, not that at all," the
militants would insist: "We are David finally standing up to
Goliath and we are going to prevail! God is on our side, we
cannot lose!" Many were persuaded. In village after village,
swords were being pulled from beneath haystacks to be pol-
ished and sharpened. Christian believers could not escape the
persuasiveness of such war-talk.

Now James, Brother of our Lord, came to rally Christians at
the Shechem Inn. He was urging them not to be seduced by the
talk of rebellion. "Ours is a kingdom devoted to peace," James
would plead. "Jesus commanded us: put aside the sword to
take up weapons of the Spirit.

> *What causes fighting and wars among you? The de-
> sire for power and goods. When nations get these,
> they only consume them on their own lusts, thus
> becoming worse off than ever. Our calling is to be
> humble, as Jesus was humble. Let God lift you up
> as he raised up Jesus, to set the world an example in*

righteous living.
You elders in the church, visit faithfully the sick
among your flocks. Pray with them and minister to
their illnesses. Confess your sins one to another, then
God will hear and heal.

I could feel the Spirit moving among the listeners as James reminded and pleaded. Many began to weep for our land and the times of great sorrow which Jesus had foretold. I recalled Jesus' own tears at Jerusalem's gates, when those cheering crowds would gladly have followed him into battle had he but lifted a sword. Instead he had pursued a battle of the soul for the redemption of mankind.

Back to their villages James' listeners went, ready to witness as they could and die if they must. Across the countryside the rumblings of war, far from ebbing, grew louder still.

Vespasian

Over and over, our town-crier announced the warning at Shechem's main crossing:

Field Marshal Vespasian and 10,000 of Rome's forces
have assembled in Lebanon. They have begun their
move southward toward Jerusalem. Shechem resi-
dents are advised to evacuate the village immediately!

I had already made up my mind, I would not leave. The Inn would be needed as a place of healing for the wounded. Our calling was to serve where the Spirit had stationed us. Many a time I had speculated with Tom, "If faced with death once more, will I measure up? Will I have the courage then that I have so often lacked?" "One never knows," Tom had always replied, "until we look the grim reaper himself in the eye."

I was writing at my registry desk, when we heard the thudding rhythm of the Roman forward units. Presently the inn's door was kicked open and in strode a Roman officer of senior rank. His eyes swept the place. Then waving a small baton in my direction, he demanded, "Are you Levi Matthew, the proprietor?"

I nodded but said nothing. "This inn" he went on, "is being taken over by Field Marshal Vespasian and his general staff. Your workers will make all rooms ready for immediate occupancy. You yourself will follow me outside to receive further orders from the Field Marshal himself. Do I make myself clear?"

Unsure, I hesitated. The man spun to look me directly into the eye. "Fool," he shouted, "can you hear me? Do you understand?"

"Sir," I answered softly, "the place is small and humble. First I must consult the owner."

"Jewish pig!" he bellowed. "The Field Marshal has not come a thousand miles to bargain with a Jewish pig!"

His eyes flashed fire. He took one last stride toward me, his face thrust almost into mine, his hand clutching the sword at his side. I could see the blood-vessels in his neck bulge and throb.

In that moment my answer came clear. "I do not hate this Roman; he has come to my door seeking shelter. He threatens me and believes he is doing what he must. If the Field Marshal and his staff do set up quarters here, I will share with them a way of life far nobler than they have ever known. God may yet use this humble inn to re-draw battle plans, beat swords into plowshares, and forge spears into pruning hooks. All who stop at the Inn of Friendships Renewed will find a welcome."

My eyes were brimming now with tears of high excitement. Through them I saw not so much this blustering Roman officer, as that young preacher from Nazareth, standing at my desk in the Capernaum tax office. Had not I heard him call, "Levi Matthew, follow me?" Why, I wondered, would a righteous preacher like him possibly seek out a tax collector like me?

> *I will go with him! My plans will be put on hold. I will follow him to discover the ways of his new and righteous Kingdom!*

Not so much as glancing down, I closed my book and placed it to the side. I did not feel the Roman sword as it entered my heart.

I followed him out onto the road.

I followed my Lord into the new and righteous Kingdom — that Kingdom whose glories are yet to be revealed and whose stories still wait to be told.

This imagined narrative combines thoughts from the First Letter of Peter, Letters of Paul (in particular, To the Romans) and the Letter of James.

ACKNOWLEDGEMENTS

Dr. Richard R. Caemmerer, beloved seminary professor, used to say, "The Bible is a book about forgiveness – check me out." During sixty years of sharing the Bible's stories in parishes across the country, at military bases, and in schools of East Asia, I have seen good things happen in the lives of listeners. People have come to believe more strongly that God wants to forgive them and that they themselves are equipped to forgive others. Writing this book at age 90 has given me one more chance to "shake the tree but lightly," with confidence that one more apronful of good things remains to be gathered.

To those who have offered encouragement along the way, I want to say a hearty thank you: especially to Bill Buege, Marie Schroeder, Dr. Fred and Lois Danker, Jim Wire, Pastor William and Valerie Yancey and others at Bethel Lutheran Church, University City, MO, our home congregation. And to all the members of my family who have been more than generous with their time and suggestions.

Jim Balogh has graciously contributed the portrait for the back cover (jim@imakepix.com). Jim is a St. Louis free-lance photographer, also a fellow worker on Habitat for Humanity projects.

Sister Marion Honors, CSJ, has graciously offered use of her wood-cut "Homecoming" for the front cover and section title-pages (marionchonorscsj@hotmail.com). Sister Marion is illustrator of numerous books. Her art work in various media has been exhibited nationally and internationally. She is a member of Sisters of St. Joseph of Carondelet, Latham, NY.

Quotations for these story retellings are for the most part my own free paraphrases based on various Bible translations. They most closely follow the Revised Standard Version of 1962, Oxford University Press.

The individual retellings may be used without further permission in not-for-profit teaching or worship situations, provided due credit is given to the book and author.

For readers wishing to share their own present-day stories of forgiveness, a sequel to this book is contemplated. Please see web site "FORGIVENESSPOSSIBLE.COM."

Thank you all for reading!

A. Karl Boehmke
Clayton, Missouri
Thanksgiving Day 2009

ABOUT THE AUTHOR

Rev. August Karl Boehmke was born in Buffalo, NY. He studied at various church colleges and seminaries, receiving master's degrees from Concordia Seminary, St. Louis, Lutheran School of Theology, Chicago, and Yale Divinity School.

He served mission congregations in Washington, DC, Detroit, MI,and Rochester, NY; also at Church of All Nations, Hong Kong. He served as chaplain in the U.S. Air Force Reserve for 28 years, on active duty during the Korean War and Cuba Crisis. He led retreats in the U.S. and Republic of Philippines. He has been active in world relief projects, Refugee resettlement and Habitat for Humanity.

He and wife, LaVerne Telle of St. Louis, are parents of three children. They live in retirement in Clayton, MO, a suburb of St. Louis.